70 ¢

D0366020

Total Church Life

Exalt • Equip • Evangelize

Darrell W. Robinson

Church Growth Strategy

FOREWORD BY
BILLY GRAHAM

BROADMAN & HOLMAN PUBLISHERS

Nashville, Tennessee

4262-50

ISBN: 0-8054-6250-3

Dewey Decimal Classification: 254

Subject Headings: CHURCH // CHURCH ADMINISTRATION

Library of Congress Card Catalog Number: 85-7900

Printed in the United States of America

Unless otherwise stated, all Scripture quotations are from the *King James Version.*

Scripture quotations marked NIV are from the Holy Bible, *New International Version,* copyright © 1973, 1978, 1984 by International Bible Society.

Library of Congress Cataloging-in-Publication Data

Robinson, Darrell W., 1935-
   Total church life.
     Bibliography:
   1. Church 2. Evangelistic work. 3. Church
management. I. Title.
BV600.2.R598 1985 262'.22

                                  85-7900

Dedication

This book is dedicated to the pastors and people of churches that have proven the New Testament principles for evangelistic growth incorporated in the Total Church Life strategy. I am grateful to the countless pastors and churches that have implemented these principles contextually. They have demonstrated the effectiveness of a comprehensive approach to evangelistic church growth. They have modeled the New Testament priorities of total penetration by a church of its area with the gospel through the involvement of total participation of its membership in witness.

It is, also, dedicated to my wife and partner in ministry, Kathleen Kyzar Robinson. Through her love and commitment she has joined me in the implementation of these principles through our life of pastoral, denominational, and kingdom ministry.

Contents

Acknowledgements

I would like to express my deep appreciation for many who have impacted my life and have assisted in the development of the Total Church Life strategy:

My pastor, Mark Reeves, who is now with our Lord, taught and practiced the principles of New Testament church life; my lifelong friend, Roy Fish, who has modeled, preached, and taught effectively New Testament evangelism; professors, pastors, and church members who have had a vision for reaching people for Christ; Robert Witty, who encouraged and instructed me in the discipline of writing; the evangelism staff of the Southern Baptist Home Mission Board who have worked as a team in making Total Church Life the foundational strategy of their work; Bobby Sunderland and Ken Carter, who have had the lead role in developing the field servicing; Thomas Wright, who edited the revised text and guided in developing support materials and products; Home Mission Board Communication Division who have assisted in development of support materials and products; secretaries Jean Smith and Virginia Whitehead, who diligently typed and proofed copies of material. Total Church Life materials are the result of the cooperative efforts of many of God's gifted people.

Foreword

The situation in the organized and institutional church today is in danger. We may be losing the battle for the minds of men and women through materialism and secularism. Unless the trend is radically reversed, the institutional church may well go into a decline. One of the problems is that the average person has little concept of what the true church really is.

Dr. Darrell Robinson has addressed that trend by accurately setting forth biblical principles of total church life. The Total Church Life strategy teaches the church's function as a body of Christ under His headship, Exalting the Savior, Equipping the Saints, and Evangelizing the Sinner. The book includes a practical application chapter called Envision the Strategy. This strategy can help any church to fulfill its evangelistic purpose.

Dr. Robinson and the evangelism staff of the Southern Baptist Home Mission Board have seen this strategy transform the lives and witness of hundreds of churches of all sizes and cultural backgrounds. The institutional church of today can avoid decline by utilizing the most effective technology but must primarily get back to the vision of New Testament evangelism.

Billy Graham

Introduction
to the Revised Edition

Total Church Life focuses on the nature of the local church in the New Testament. It sets forth biblical principles of evangelistic church growth based on the conviction that what church *does* grows out of what church *is*. The foundation of true church growth is Christ Himself and His mission for the church, His body.

The book's title, *Total Church Life,* expresses the necessity for a mind-set of evangelistic growth to permeate every church organization and activity. The church grows effectively when it functions as a health body of Christ with each member actively involved in obedience to its head.

The Total Church Life strategy has been used by churches of every size, culture, and life-style. Many are experiencing evangelistic growth as they apply and implement the principles to develop an evangelism strategy. In the process suggestions have come from the field and have been added to this new edition. The revised edition places more emphasis on how to plan and implement an evangelism strategy in the local church. Chapter 10 has a new name, "Envision the Strategy," and includes specific helps to apply the strategy in any church regardless of size or ethnic background.

I pray the Lord will continue to use the Total Church Life evangelism strategy as a catalyst to stimulate churches to develop a comprehensive strategy for evangelizing our nation for Jesus Christ.

Introduction:

Let the Church Be the Church

Our world has all but forgotten what church is all about. So have many churches. The greatest need in our time is a first-century church in a twenty-first-century world. It is time that the church returned to the principles of the New Testament. Let the church be the church with a vision from God for its mission.

The greatest need of our time is not economic, social, political, or ecological. The greatest need of our generation is for the church to be the church. Through the powerful spiritual and moral influence of dynamic churches, these problems would be resolved.

D. L. Moody, the great evangelist of the nineteenth century, overheard someone say, "The world has yet to see what God can do through one man whose life is totally committed to Him."

Moody said, "I will be that man."[1]

Through Moody's life, multitudes were converted to God. Two continents were shaken for Christ. His work continues to bear fruit until this very moment.

When I read the testimony of D. L. Moody, God gripped my heart. First, He challenged my own life to total commitment. Then, He impressed me to apply this same truth to a local church—to a body of believing people.

It was as if God were saying to me, "Our world, at least in this generation, has yet to see what God can do through the life of a local church, a body of believers in Christ totally committed to Him."

This is a body of people who do not ask, "Can we do it?"

They simply ask, "God, what do You want us to do?

They do not ask, "What will it cost? Have we ever done it before?"

They simply ask, "God, what do You want us to do? We know You will supply the resources for all You desire us to do."

By faith they launch out with the flexibility and creativity to obey God. With confidence that God will supply the resources for all He desires done, they move forward by faith.

God moved my heart to challenge the church I pastored to be that church. The people responded with joy and enthusiasm. Revival came. God began to do mighty things.

As a church begins the adventure of being a first-century church in a twenty-first-century world, the reality of what it means to be a church must be considered. What a church does is determined by what a church is.

The Nature of Church

The word *church* in the New Testament comes from the Greek term *ekklesia*. It comes from a root word made up of a preposition *ek* (out of) and a verb *kaleo* (to call). *Ekkaleo* means "to call out of."[2]

Church, *ekklesia,* refers to those who have been called out from sin to salvation. They have been touched by their Lord. They are set apart for Him and for His service. They are a distinctive people on mission for their Lord in this world.

In the New Testament the word *church* is used one hundred fifteen times. Twenty times it is used in a general sense to refer to the total body of redeemed, the saved of all ages. Ninety-five times it is used in a local sense to refer to a local congregation of believing people.[3]

First, in a general sense there is one church. It is not an

organization—it is an organism. It does not have organic unity—it has spiritual unity.[4]

The general church includes every believer who has ever lived. It includes those born-again people from every denomination, every nationality, every background, and culture in this world.

The general church is spoken of in Ephesians 5:32— "This is a great mystery: but I speak concerning Christ and the church." The word *church* here speaks of that total body of redeemed people. All who belong to Jesus Christ belong to the general church of our Lord.

What a blessed thing it is that we have spiritual unity with brothers and sisters in Christ wherever we go. We may meet them on the other side of the earth, but we are one. We are indwelt by the Lord Jesus Christ. We are brothers and sisters in the family of our Lord. These are those who will be caught up together with Him in the clouds when Jesus comes again. It will be one church in heaven with Him. That will be glory! We will sit together in heavenly places in Christ Jesus. Amen!

The word *church* is used twenty times in the general sense. But the great thrust of the New Testament is on the local church. The word is used almost five times as often in a local sense.

It is the local church that gives practical expression to the teachings of our Lord Jesus Christ. It is the local church that carries out the mission and ministry of our Lord Jesus Christ.[5] In 1 Corinthians 1:2 Paul wrote, "Unto the church of God which is at Corinth"—an individual local church. In Galatians 1:2 Paul again wrote, "Unto the churches of Galatia." The word *church* is plural, referring to numerous local bodies of believers. In Revelation 1:4 the Lord Jesus spoke to John about "the seven churches" in Asia. There is not just one church visibly and organically. There are many local churches. The mission of the local churches is to bring people to Jesus and into the general Body of Christ. That mission is the same in congregations of every language and culture.

A Definition of a Local Church

Wherever you may go, you will see buildings with signs in front. First Church, Community Church, etc. But the church is not buildings; it uses buildings. The church is not organization; it uses organization. It is not programs, although it uses programs.

Church is people: people who have received their life from Jesus Christ, people who are sharing that life with one another, people who are extending the Christ-life to all those about them. Church is: people sharing Jesus!

But we live in a day of the *building* mentality. When I said to my wife, "I am going down to the church," I was wrong. I should have said, "I am going to the building where the church meets." Without thinking, we use the term incorrectly. We betray a *building* mentality.

Church is people. The people of God could meet in a tent, in the park under a tree, in homes, in a school building, or wherever and still be the church.

The definition of a local church my former pastor taught me years ago is this: "A local church is a body of baptized believers in Jesus Christ who have banded together to carry out the commission of Jesus Christ."

Each word of the definition is important. A church is a *body,* drawn together by our Lord unto Himself. It is a *body of believers* in Jesus Christ. They have voluntarily, without coercion, banded together through their mutual faith and trust in the person of Jesus Christ.[6]

They are baptized unto Him. Baptism is the outward identification of each believer with Jesus Christ and with one another. There can be no such thing as a secret Christian. The faith of a Christian is to be open, verbally confessed.

The purpose of believers coming together as a church is to carry out the mission of Jesus in His world. What Jesus came to do, He left His church to continue to accomplish.

> Go ye therefore, and teach all nations, baptizing them in the name of the Father, and of the Son, and of the Holy Ghost: Teaching them to observe all things whatsoever I have commanded you: and, lo, I am with you alway, even unto the end of the world (Matt. 28:19-20).

The Primacy of the Local Church

The New Testament strongly emphasizes the local church. I feel the local church is the most important single factor on this earth. In the Book of Revelation Jesus is seen walking in the midst of His churches. He chose, through local churches, to permeate this world with His teachings and life.

Second only to Jesus Himself, the apostle Paul is the leading figure of the New Testament. He wrote thirteen of its books. He journeyed through the Roman Empire evangelizing. He is responsible—perhaps more than any other man—for the spread of Christianity.

What was Paul's priority? He evangelized people and congregationalized them into local churches. These churches were hubs for the evangelization of their areas. Paul established no schools. He started no hospitals. He instituted no social ministries. These are important in our world and in the work of the Lord. But these and other ministries are the results of alive, functioning local churches.

As local churches begin to practice the Christ-life, compassion, concern, and interest in the lives of people develop. From this kind of concern come educational, social, medical, and other ministries to meet the needs of the total person and the total community.

The local church is primary today. Many who live in communities where local churches are strong take them for granted. One has only to go where local churches are weak to see a distinct difference in the climate of the community. The influence of a strong local church increases the moral and spiritual vitality of the community and deepens concern for individuals.

In these days, every kind of attack is being launched against the church. Every kind of evil is being hurled against it. Fingers of accusation are pointed from every direction. Some are saying, "We do not need the church. The church is outdated." But Jesus' plan for the church remains unchanged. He has built the church upon the rock of His own lordship and the gates of hell shall not prevail against it. The church will be here when Jesus comes back. It will not only survive, it will march forward to victory!

It is better to serve God in the life of a local church than to do any other thing in this earth. It is better to be a part of a local church of our living Lord Jesus and join hands with Him in the adventure He has for us today than to do anything else.

There is no reason to hang our heads in despair with eyes looking downward and spirits low. It is time to look up to the heavens "from whence cometh" our help (Ps. 121:1). The church must look up to Jesus. He is coming again! When He comes, He will call His victorious church to Himself.

Jesus is the head of the church, His body. He has put all things under His feet. His feet are a part of His body. A local church filled with the life of Jesus Christ walks in victory over this present world.

The church is the bride of Jesus Christ. Husbands are admonished to love their wives as Christ loved His church and gave Himself for it. He sanctifies and cleanses it with the washing of water by His Word (Eph. 5:25-27). Jesus loves His church.

Some people say, "I love Jesus, but I don't have any use for the church." This is totally inconsistent! One cannot love Jesus without loving what Jesus loves. Jesus loves His church. Those who claim to believe in Jesus but attack His church must take heed. You do not attack a man's bride without incurring his wrath. Jesus will not long tolerate a person's attack against His bride. Judgment on such behavior is certain!

The Prospect of the Church

Our Lord will present His church to Himself without spot or wrinkle. But the church today is not without fault. It is not pure white. It is spotted and wrinkled. But when Jesus comes again, He will present His church to Himself in radiant glory like a bride to her husband. Paul uses the analogy of a pure white garment, pressed and ironed without wrinkle.[7] How can the church become a glistening white instead of a drab, dingy gray? How can the church be presented without wrinkle? A garment is washed clean through agitation. The wrinkles are pressed out through heat and pressure. The church of our Lord is under the agitation of attack. From every direction there is turmoil and opposition stirred by Satan. It is under the pressure and heat of the attack of Satan and his followers. Jesus is preparing the church for Himself without spot or wrinkle.

The Purpose of a Local Church

The purpose of a church is to be the body of Christ—filled with the Christ-life. It is a Christ-filled body, living in a community, radiating the glory of the indwelling presence of Jesus. It becomes the light of the world and the salt of the earth. The rays of its light penetrate into every sin-darkened strata of a moral and spiritual life of a community. Its pungent influence permeates a society. A church is to be a local body of Christ.

Analogy of the Body (2 Cor.5:1-4)

Why did Paul choose to use the analogy of a human body as a metaphor to reveal the relationship between Christ and

His church? What relationship do you have with your body that provides an analogy for the relationship between Christ and His body, the church? The answer is seen in 2 Corinthians 5:1-4. There we are told that our body is an earthly house, a tabernacle that will be dissolved. When this happens, we will have a building of God, a house not made with hands, eternal in the heavens.

Your body is a temporary dwelling place. You live in it for awhile. Death will come. You will move out into the house God has promised for you in heaven. This body is an earthly home. For those who know Jesus Christ there is an eternal house, a permanent one, prepared by the Father in heaven.

I have explained it to our church with this illustration. One of these days you will get word that I have died. Now, that is a morbid thought, unless you are a Christian. But when you get that word, you will come down to the church building for a funeral. You will see them wheeling me in, in a box. They will bring it down the aisle to the front to the church house.

In many of our churches the people have the custom of walking by and viewing the body after the sermon. I can see it all now. After whatever is to be said has been said, everyone will walk by and look in. I can hear them now.

"Oh, my, look at Brother Darrell. Doesn't he look natural?"

Natural, my foot! I will be dead!

When that happens, do not mourn, weep, cry, and carry on. At least, not a whole lot. Some, maybe! (I surely wouldn't want to die without anyone caring.) But when you look in, remember, that is not me. I will not be there. I will have moved out. That is just the house I lived in for awhile. I will have moved out to be with Jesus. I will have already gone where I was headed. I will have received what I lived for; I will be with Jesus, having the time of my life.

Death for the Christian is not a sorrowful ending. It is the glorious transition of receiving the fullness of all God has for us. It is the only perfect healing. All earthly healing is temporary. God may even heal us, but we get sick again. One of these days, one of those sicknesses is going to get us. We are going to die. However, when God takes us home to be with Him forever, that perfect healing is eternal.

This body is the house we live in for a little while. Through it we think, live, move, and function. What is the church? Like your body provides a house within which you live, the church collectively—and believers individually—provide a house within which Jesus comes to live in this world.

> What? know ye not that your body is the temple of the Holy Ghost which is in you, which ye have of God, and ye are not your own? For ye are bought with a price: therefore glorify God in your body, and in your spirit, which are God's (1 Cor. 6:19-20).
>
> That Christ may dwell in your hearts by faith (Eph. 3:17).

Jesus has taken up His residence in His body, the church. He comes personally to indwell every believer. Individually and collectively, the church is the body of Jesus Christ. He lives in us. What a glorious reality!

> Now unto him that is able to do exceeding abundantly above all that we ask or think according to the power that worketh in us, Unto him be glory in the church by Christ Jesus throughout all ages, world without end (Eph. 3:20-21).

Jesus is glorified in His church as He dwells in it. He fills it with all His fullness. He does exceeding abundantly above all that we can ask or think. What potential! The life of Jesus Christ is reproduced in and through His body, the church.

Two Perspectives of Church

There are two perspectives of the church as the body of Christ. First, it is the body of Christ *gathered.* Second, it is the body of Christ *scattered.*[8]

First, the many members of the local church body gather together. If I were to ask you where your church is located, you would have to answer with a question—When?

On Sunday morning, a local church is meeting together in buildings dedicated for that purpose. It is doing so in obedience to the Lord's command, because of the need of individual members, and because of the necessity for doing so in carrying out the mission of Jesus.

> Let us hold fast the profession of our faith without wavering; (for he is faithful that promised;) And let us consider one another to provoke unto love and to good works: Not forsaking the assembling of ourselves together, as the manner of some is; but exhorting one another: and so much the more, as ye see the day approaching (Heb. 10:23-25).

The church comes together to lift up Jesus in praise, joy, and worship. The Holy Spirit moves in a unique and wonderful way. Where two or three are gathered in His name, there is He in the midst of them. As the church gathers, He moves to strengthen, energize, guide, and direct through the instruction of His Word. He inspires and fills His people. God's people come together to encourage one another. We are told to consider one another, to provoke one another to love and good works. Every Christian needs that. Every Christian needs to be admonished and encouraged, prodded and provoked to love and good works. The church gathers for worship, instruction, proclamation of the Word, fellowship, equipping, and training.

In the modern world, many are negative about attending church. A hostile world snarls at those who come together "behind stained-glass windows." The world says that it can worship God as well at home, in the mountains, or on the creek bank as it can in church. That might be true. But the fact is, they do not do so. Those who truly worship our Lord in private will also obey Him in corporate worship.

Much of the world is negative about the organized church

and its buildings. Buildings and organizations are not primary. The church is people. But a meeting place is necessary. The building provides a base of operation.

From the very earliest time when God called out a people, He gathered them together. When He brought His people out of Egypt through the wilderness, they lived in tents. He instructed them to build a beautiful tabernacle. It was the most beautiful tent in all the camp of Israel. They were to bring their best. They were to build the tabernacle out of the best they had. As they came together to worship in the beautiful tabernacle, it was the glory spot in their camp.

When Israel inherited the land of promise, God gave them instructions for building the temple. It was a beautiful, magnificent structure.

Early Christians met first in homes. As congregations grew, they moved to larger homes and eventually built their own buildings for worship. We need to remember that the church must not be building centered but people centered. Buildings within which God's people meet are used for His glory. They serve as a constant reminder to a community that God is at work in the lives of people.

Second, the church is the body of Christ scattered. Where is your church? On Sunday morning it is gathered together in the building dedicated for its meeting place. But if gathering is all the church does, it defeats the mission of Jesus in this earth.

What about Monday morning? Where is your church? Meeting in the buildings? No! Your church is scattered to the four winds. Everywhere a member of your church goes, there goes the church. Jesus is living in that person to do again all that He did when He was here in the flesh. He is here in the flesh of that person. Throughout the week your church is scattered through its community, area, state, nation, and to the ends of the earth. Everywhere it goes, there goes Jesus Christ ministering to people, touching people, bringing them to God. There goes Jesus in and through His people—into homes, businesses, schools, neighborhoods, government buildings, and social gatherings.

What glorious potential! Tremendous! If a church will understand and practice this reality, it will literally transform its community. A church so filled with the Christ-life will penetrate its entire community with the witness of Jesus. It will be said of them as was said of the early Christians: "These that have turned the world upside down are come hither also" (Acts 17:6).

This is what happened in the early church. Upon the persecution of Stephen, God scattered the church. Multitudes had been saved in Jerusalem. They were rejoicing in the Lord. But Jesus meant for them to evangelize their city, Judea, Samaria, and the uttermost part of the earth. They were not doing it.

God scattered the church. Everyone left Jerusalem except the preachers. The preachers stayed at the hub of things in Jerusalem. But God scattered the people. The Scripture says that they went *everywhere* preaching (see Acts 8:1).

The church gathers for strengthening, scatters for service. The church gathers for worship, scatters for witness. The church gathers in praise, scatters in power. The church gathers in fellowship, scatters in faith following its Lord. The church gathers to equip the saints, scatters to evangelize the sinner.

This is the function of the church: simply to be the body of Jesus Christ. Functioning as the body of Christ, the church has three priorities. We will discuss these three priorities in the following pages.

The Priorities of the Local Church

First, the church as the body of Christ will *exalt the Savior*. Jesus is the Head of the church, His body. He is to have the preeminence. We are to lift Him up in all things—exalt the Savior.

Second, the church will *equip the saints*. The church, the

called-out ones, must be equipped to live the Christ-life and to extend His life to others. When God's people are equipped, they will do the work of the ministry and build up the body of Christ—equip the Saints.

Third, the church will *evangelize the sinner.* If Christ is exalted, if the people of God are equipped for the ministry; then, the church will reach the lost. The mission of Jesus in our world is to seek and to save that which is lost. If a church is His body, He lives within. His mission becomes our mission. As beats the heart of Jesus, so beats the heart of His body, the church—evangelize the sinner.

This is what church is all about. The threefold priority of the church is: exalt the Savior, equip the saints, and evangelize the sinner. A church cannot do one of these without doing all three. If, indeed, it is doing one of them, it will be doing all three. The application of these priorities is described in chapter 10: "Envision the Strategy."

At this point churches face a great danger. Some find it more comfortable to attempt to do one of these to the exclusion of the others. To do so causes a church to become unbalanced. It develops a lopsided kind of ministry that ultimately leads to heresy.

For instance, some may decide to be an exalt-the-Savior church—a praise-the-Lord church. The church comes together and enjoys lifting up Jesus and praising the Lord. If the lost get saved, God can do that! They do not have a real passion for the lost. But, there is something lacking here. We cannot truly exalt the Savior and lift Him up without a real passion for the lost. He came to seek and to save that which is lost. If indeed, He is our Lord, His passion will be our passion.

Others may concentrate on the deeper life. How we need to go deeper in Jesus! The deeper life movement is tremendous. But it is only part of the great thrust of a Scriptural church. It is the blessed part, but only one part.

Some may decide to be an equipping church. They do not

feel comfortable with outreach. They are suspicious of much praise and joy. They decide to develop quality Christians instead of quantity. They say, "There may not be many of us, but we are developing the best." What a deception! If we are truly being equipped, it is for the purpose of living the Christ-life and sharing Him with others.

Still others decide to be an evangelism church. Every time they meet, the message is the plan of salvation with different illustrations. Many people may make professions of faith and come into the church. But the people are not equipped nor deepened in the Christ-life.

True evangelism is not a program. It is a result. It is the result of the church being a life-filled body of Christ—exalting the Savior, equipping believers to live the Christ-life and to share Him with others.

Jesus is the Head of the church. When He is lifted up, His life fills the body so that the people of God are equipped with power to utilize their gifts to fulfill His mission in the earth. Evangelism, then, is the natural consequence of a living church. The church uses programs and activities, but evangelism is its life-style.

Evangelism is the outflow of the overflow of the inflow of the Christ-life within the church.

Questions

1. What is meant by the statement, "Total Church Life is not a program. It's a strategy"? Why is Total Church more effective as a strategy?

2. What do you hope to gain personally from Total Church Life?

3. If you were a medical doctor, how would you describe the health of your church?

4. What is the threefold priority of the church? How does it apply to your church?

5. What is one way you hope Total Church Life will help your church?

1 Exalt the Savior:

Through the Body Life of the Church

"And he is the head of the body, the church: who is the beginning, the firstborn from the dead; that in all things he might have the preeminence" (Col. 1:18).

Paul uses the analogy of a human body to show the relationship between Christ and His church. The body has two parts: Head and body. Jesus is the Head. The church is His body. The body depends upon the Head for its life.

In the Vine-branch relationship in John 15, the life of the Vine flows through the branches. The branches depend upon the Vine. They abide in the Vine. In like manner, the Head sustains the body. The body exalts the Savior, the Head, the Lord Jesus.

The Headship of Jesus

Jesus is Lord. His headship over the church has been established by His intervention in human history. He founded the church. He directs and sustains the function of the church. He controls the future of the church.

As Head, Jesus is to be lifted up. "And I, if I be lifted up from the earth, will draw all men unto me" (John 12:32). How do you reach people for Christ? Lift up Jesus! It is He who draws persons to Himself.

Jesus Has Been Lifted Up

First, He has been lifted up on the cross! They drove nails through His hands and feet. He was smitten of God and afflicted. He was bruised for our iniquities, and the chastisement of our peace was upon Him. He bore our sins in His own body on the tree. God made Him, who knew no sin, to be sin for us. God laid upon Him the iniquity of us all.

At the cross, God did a miracle. He reached out through all human history to every individual. He took all the sin of every person who would ever live and concentrated the guilt of all sin into the body of His Son. Jesus paid in full the penalty for all our sins.

Our sins killed Him. He did not die from the wounds in His hands and feet. Medical technicians indicate that the presence of blood and water which flowed from His pierced side indicate that His heart had ruptured. The agony of our sins killed Him. He died for our sins.

"It is finished" was a shout of triumph, not the words of a dejected, defeated Man. The plan of God for human redemption was accomplished. The way for people to enter into the presence of God was made. The sin debt had been paid, in full, for humanity. Thank God! He has been lifted up that we might be forgiven and freed from the penalty of sin.

Second, He has been lifted up from the grave. They took Him down from the cross and laid Him in the grave. They rolled a great stone over the mouth of the tomb. They sealed it with a Roman seal. They set a guard upon it. He was dead! They would keep Him dead!

But all the forces of earth and hell could not keep Jesus in the tomb. On the third day, by the mighty power of God, Jesus came forth from the dead to guarantee resurrection power for victorious living to every person who would receive Him.

His dejected disciples had scattered. But after the resurrection, Jesus showed Himself to them alive from the dead by many infallible proofs. For forty days He met with them; He gave them instructions and commands. He carefully commissioned them to share His gospel with every person.

He has been lifted up to the right hand of God. His disciples gathered with Him on the Mount of Olives. He gave them final words of instruction for world evangelization. "When he had spoken these things, while they beheld, he was taken up; and a cloud received him out of their sight" (Acts 1:9). He took His place in authority at the right hand of the Father. He ever lives to make intercession for all who come to God through Him (Heb. 7:25).

Now, through Him we can come boldly to the throne of grace to obtain mercy and find grace in time of need (Heb. 4:14-16). We have access into the very throne room of the Creator of this universe, our Father. He has been lifted up!

Jesus Will Be Lifted Up

Jesus is coming again! He will descend from heaven with a shout, with the voice of an archangel and the trumpet of God. When He comes, the dead in Christ will be raised from the grave. Those who are alive and remain will be caught up together with Him in the clouds. We will ever be with the Lord. Moreover, He will be lifted up in His mighty power as King of kings and Lord of lords. Then, every knee shall bow, and every tongue confess Him as Lord to the glory of God the Father (Phil. 2:11). So there is no room for discouragement, no room for defeat in the life of the Christian. We must keep our eyes lifted upward. He is coming again. He is King of kings and Lord of lords. Live His victory today! He has been lifted up, and He will be lifted up. This is the work of God.

The Church Must Lift Him Up Today

Today it remains for you and me to lift Him up here on earth. He said, "I, if I be lifted up from the earth, will draw all men unto me" (John 12:32). As you and I lift Him up before people, He does draw them to Himself.

How are we to win souls? How are people's lives to be changed? By lifting up Jesus. That is the way it happens. We want to see the church grow. We want to see it filled with mighty power. We want to see people drawn to Jesus. We want to see lives strengthened. *Lift up Jesus!* He is Head of the church, His body. We must lift Him up.

He Has Preeminence (Col. 1:18)

Headship is absolute! There can be no equal. There cannot be two heads governing one body. There is one Head: *Jesus!* This is lordship. Jesus is Lord of the church.

There can be no rival. Jesus is Head of the church. He will tolerate no rival.[1] The source of most church trouble is when some human personality begins to lift up self to compete with Jesus for headship. When this happens, there is trouble in the church. The fellowship of the church will disintegrate. Anytime an individual or group within the church begins to rival Jesus for headship, there is trouble. Jesus will tolerate no rival.

Headship is a theocracy. Humanly, in organization, the church is a democracy. Each member of a local church may vote personal expression of conviction. But, spiritually, a local church is a theocracy under the headship of Jesus. The right way for the church to conduct itself is to seek His will, come together and vote to do His will, and then do it.

There is no place for division in the body. Members should not determine what they want, then campaign to build group support for their will. There is no excuse for factions competing with one another in the church to get their way.

Trouble comes when some strong-willed person says, "I will have my way or else!" Churches usually do not have trouble over something important. It is usually over some insignificant thing: somebody's pet peeve, somebody's special desire—over what color the carpet is going to be, whether we're going to have cushions on the pews or not, or how we are going to spend a few dollars.

When I was a student pastor, I learned a valuable lesson about this. There was a church fuss in business meeting one night. It was over an old piano. The church piano was out of tune. The piano tuner said it was beyond hope. The keys would stick. Dirt daubers had built nests in the back. We located a better piano for one hundred dollars. We could sell the old one for fifty. The proposal was presented. It would cost the church fifty dollars.

Then the discussion started. An angry cowboy stood and said, "I don't know why the preacher wants us to buy another piano. This piano has been a good 'un. It's been good enough for us for years."

Somebody else responded. Before I knew what was happening, a quarrel was going. The cowboy got up and stormed out. I can still hear his cowboy boots clicking on the wood floor all the way to the door. He stood out on the porch fuming mad.

I asked the people to spend some time in prayer while I went out to talk with him. I asked him to come in, pray, seek the mind of the Lord, vote, and do the will of the majority.

When we came back inside, a blessed deacon saved the day. He was the only deacon in the little church. He was a true deacon. He poured oil on troubled waters. He stood up and spoke, "Brothers and Sisters, you know this has been a good ole piano. We've had it for fifty years. We gave fifty dollars for it back then. We have surely got our money's worth out of it. Now it is time we upgraded a bit. It will only cost fifty dollars for a newer one. Why don't we go ahead and get it?"

By the time we were ready to vote, even the cowboy voted for it. Together we went forward. We had a good meeting. It is usually those little things which flare up that bring trouble in the church. It happens when we start promoting and pushing our own opinion and desires rather than seeking the Lord.

The Head Is to Be Obeyed

Having a sign over the door naming it "church" does not make it a New Testament church. If we are truly to follow the New Testament, we must submit to the lordship of Jesus, our Head. For a church to follow the New Testament, it must be New Testament in principle and in practice, in belief and in behavior, in doctrine and in duty.

A church may "believe" all the right things and still not be a New Testament church. It may be sound in its adoption of the right doctrines of the Scripture, yet be far from scriptural in its conduct. It may claim the right beliefs, yet not practice them.

Jesus warned the church at Ephesus in Revelation 2:5 to repent and do again the first works. Otherwise, He would remove its candlestick from out of its place. We are to practice the attitude and mission of Jesus as well as hold to the right doctrine.

If a church fails to fulfill the mission of Jesus—no matter what it says its doctrine is—it is no more New Testament than some religious country club or social group. There is always pressure to forsake the true mission of the church. There is always the temptation for a church to turn its eyes inward, to think only of itself. A church may settle back in comfort with members simply enjoying themselves rather than reaching their world for Christ.

This was what had happened in our county-seat-town church. It was the largest church in the area. It had a history of reaching people, yet the people's attitude toward missions had changed. The church declined to about half the size it had once been, then the vision of the church began to revive. We began to apply the principles of Jesus in reaching out from the church building into all areas of the community. We divided the town into four quarters. We began to saturate each quarter with the gospel of Christ. People began to come from every neighborhood. Among them were rich and poor; black, brown, and white; educated and uneducated. It was becoming a church of the people. Several black people came. Both adults and young people received Christ and were baptized. One young black man surrendered to the gospel ministry.

Just before the deacons' meeting one Sunday afternoon, one of our fine, older deacons asked to speak to me. He loved the church with all his heart. He was his pastor's friend. He had invested his life in the church. He was a man of God. But he was disturbed. He believed his church was being threatened.

"Pastor," he said to me urgently, "we must do something! We have problems!"

"What are they?" I asked. "I am not aware of any great problem. Tell me about it."

"It is those . . ." (his term for African-American people). "They are ruining our church! Some of our members are disturbed. Two of our men, who are big givers, have talked to me about it. They say that they are going to quit coming. They say they are going to quit giving. They say that they give a lot, that it will really hurt our church. They say that when we sing our fellowship song and reach out to join hands, they will not join hands with a . . . ."

They did quit giving. It really hurt! However, the church's giving doubled within the next two years! God honors the church that will be shaped by His mission rather than by the attitudes of the world.

My response to my deacon friend was as follows: "We are about to have our deacons' meeting. You have every right to present this to the deacons. They can discuss it, recommend to the church for us to exclude the black people, and say that no black people can enter this church building. They can stop blacks from coming to Christ through our witness and from being baptized in our baptistry. This congregation has the freedom to exclude anyone it chooses. It might decide to also exclude the brown people. It may also decide to exclude some of the white people from certain areas of town or from a certain educational or social background. But if we do, we will be voting ourselves right out of being a New Testament church."

The troubled deacon responded, "Pastor, that is right. I know that is right. But this bothers me so much. They keep coming to me and talking to me about it."

"If they come to you again," I replied, "Share with them our discussion. You may tell them I would be happy to talk with them. Or they may present their views to the congregation. I am not here to run the congregation or to railroad anything through the church. The congregation can vote and do exactly what it decides to do. It has that freedom in the Lord. It can close its doors to anyone it chooses. But if it violates the mission of Jesus, it is wrong."

Of course, the church did not do that. The church kept on in its ministry of outreach to its city. It continued to saturate the city and grow. Jesus is Head of the church. When He is in control, the church will be New Testament both in belief and conduct. The Lord will provide for that church!

The Head Is to Be Followed

The Head is the control center. It does the thinking, directing, planning, and sets forth the strategy and purpose. It coordinates the body of members. The Head fitly joins the members together as one body. The Head establishes the vision for the body. It expresses the personality. What joy it is when the entire church body is filled with the personality of Jesus. It becomes truly the light of the world.

The Head is the unifier of the church. Jesus is the center. He draws His own into unity in Himself. There is only one reason such diverse people come together—Jesus! Background, culture, education, interests, and human goals will not bring all the people who are a part of a church body together. The only One who can bring such diverse people together is Jesus.

The unity of the church cannot be in a human personality. It cannot be in a program. Otherwise, it is superficial. When that particular program is over or that particular personality fails, the unity will disintegrate.

> For as the body is one, and hath many members, and all the members of that one body, being many, are one body: so also is Christ. For by one Spirit are we all baptized into one body, whether we be Jews or Gentiles, whether we be bond or free; and have been all made to drink into one Spirit (1 Cor. 12:12-13).

This is the purpose of the baptism of the Holy Spirit. The baptism of the Holy Spirit is not in order to give a particular gift. His work is to incorporate transformed members into the body of Christ. First, He baptizes every member into union with Jesus. Second, He baptizes every member into unity with other members in the body. He enables them to live the Christ-life. He empowers them to share the witness of the Lord Jesus. It is Jesus who makes the body one.

The Body Life of the Church

Unity of Membership

"For as the body is one, and hath many members, . . . For the body is not one member, but many" (1 Cor. 12:12-14). It is one body under one Head, Christ. Christ is not divided. Members cannot be "up" on Jesus and "down" on one another at the same time. There is power in unity. When the unity of the church disintegrates, the power is depleted. In unity a church can accomplish whatever God has for it to do. A church has only a certain amount of time, energy, and ability. If this is disoriented by confusion, it cannot focus on the mission of Jesus. If its energy is consumed in the negative attacks of members on members, there will be none left to carry out the mission of Jesus in reaching a lost world.

If a human body attempts to divide itself, it becomes disunited. It becomes disfigured, dismembered, and loses its power. It is so with a local church body. The unity of the body is necessary for effectiveness. A church can accomplish the impossible if its members are in one accord, giving their all in obedience to the mission of Jesus. There is mighty power in the concentrated effort of a united body of Christ.[2]

Unity Expressed in Worship

Under the headship of Jesus, the church comes together to exalt the Savior in the unity of worship. Christ is lifted up with joyful praise and celebrative adoration. In a warm climate of prayers, the Word of God is preached with the anointing of the Holy Spirit. The people of God give testimony to the mighty works of God. The church is strengthened and the lost are saved through Spirit-led and Spirit-filled worship of the One who has the "preeminence in all things."

Unity of worship is achieved through planning. The pastor and worship leader plan the theme of the service. The sermons, music, and readings should reflect the theme. Involve the laity: men, women, youth, and children. Include a testimony, lay-led prayers, drama presentation, or some opportunity for lay involvement in every service. The inviatation is a vital part of the service, not to be tacked on when time is gone.

Diversity of Members (1 Cor. 12:14-21)

God brings different members together according to His master plan to build up the church. There are many members in the body. The foot cannot say that it is unimportant because it is not the hand. The ear cannot minimize its importance because it is not the eye. "But now hath God set the members every one of them in the body, as it hath pleased him" (1 Cor. 12:18).

No one member can supply all the needs of the body. No one member can be the whole body. What if the whole body were one huge eye, rolling along? Where would be the hearing or the smelling? Every member is needed! Otherwise, the body becomes a cripple. If a human body had as many inactive, diseased, injured members as do many churches, it could not walk or even crawl along through life.

Every member is important! "Nay, much more those members of the body, which seem to be more feeble, are necessary" (v. 22). *Everybody* is *somebody* in the *Lord's body*. There are not any nobodies! There is no Mr. Big or Mr. Little.

Here is a life principle. God has made no two leaves on a tree alike. No two blades of grass are alike. No two snowflakes are alike. Happy is the person and the church that will accept and utilize the diversity of its members. Diversity is the key to dynamic potential.

Proper evaluation of self on the part of each member is necessary. One is not to think more highly of himself than he ought to think but to think soberly (see Rom. 12:3). Every member should be led to realize her value to the entire body. She should be led to understand that God has a ministry for each one in the body. One of the things that kept me from responding to God's call to preach was that I did not think I could. As I observed other preachers and church leaders, I knew that I could never do that. Although I was a Christian, I had never done anything in church except come, sit, and listen. When I observed someone pray aloud, teach, preach, sing, or witness, my conclusion was: "I could never do that."

My problem was: I did not consider myself religious. I saw preachers as religious talkers. I was not a talker. In school, I would not lift my hand when I knew the answer to a question. My voice trembled. But the heaviness of God's impression to preach continued to grow. When I surrendered to preach, I began to try to be like I thought other preachers were. I was miserable. Then I came to realize that many people need to be "listened to" as much as "preached at." I could listen. I found that I could listen people right into the kingdom of God by giving them some direction. God began to remove my fear. He enabled me to speak publicly.

Many of our people are living defeated lives because they think they are unimportant. They do not have the challenge to be involved in the body life of the church. Accept your uniqueness! This is the secret of contentment. Let God use your individuality in the church. This is the source of great dynamics for the church.[3]

Independence of Members (1 Cor. 12:4-10,15-17)

To some extent, each member of the body is independent from every other member of the body. Remember the analogy of the human body? The ear hears, but the eye does not. The eye sees. Each receives signals from the head to do what it does. Even so, each member receives direction from the Lord Jesus in ministry. Christ can lead one member to be involved in His service in ways of which other members are not aware. He speaks directly to each individual member. Here is a great truth! As members go about their daily routine of living, they individually serve the Lord Jesus and His church.[4]

Here, also, is a great danger—that independence can be pressed too far. While God leads members independently of one another, He never leads one to do that which is detrimental to the body or to another member. As one member acts or speaks, one is to do so to edify the entire body.

When independence is overstressed, members begin to feel that they do not need other members. They can stress their own independence to the point of detriment to the church. They can become determined to have their own way. Divisiveness and stubborn pride can develop.

In the human body the head may send a signal to the right hand to lift itself above the head without the left hand doing a thing. But, the head never sends a signal to the right hand to hit the body in the nose. The right hand and every member of the body is interested in the nose's welfare. They are members of the same body. When one member suffers, all suffer with it.

Interdependence of Members (1 Cor. 12:20-25)

Members are responsible to one another in the body. The attitude "What I do is my business and none of yours" is defeating to the body of Christ. While the Lord does lead each individual personally, what I do is your business. What you do is my business. We are part of the same body. What I do affects you. What you do affects me. We are members one of another. Members of the body are responsible for one another. Each needs the other. I need you. You need me. We are to love one another. We are to give mutual support to one another. There is an interrelationship among the members of the body. They are to have the same care one for another.

Dr. Jack McGorman, in one of his seminary lectures, told the allegory of the members of the body declaring war on the stomach. The members were doing all the work. The stomach was getting all the advantage. The mouth said, "I will not feed the stomach anymore."

What is the result of such foolish behavior? Mouth, stomach, and the whole body attend the same funeral—theirs! Churches and members need to learn this lesson. Many churches have been destroyed by violating this principle. When Christ is honored as Head of the church, He coordinates the loving care of member for member.

Gifts for Edification (1 Cor. 12:28-31; Rom. 12:6-8)

The Lord Jesus, the Head of the church, makes provision for His body. He gives gifts. Gifts are for the building up of the body so that it can fulfill the mission of its Lord. He has provided everything that is needed for any church to accomplish all that God desires of it in its world. He has gifted every church so that it can be all He desires it to be.

Gifts are given to the body. They belong to the church.

They are to be used to edify or build up the body. "But now hath God set the members every one of them in the body, as it hath pleased him" (1 Cor. 12:18). While gifts are distributed through each member of the body, they belong to the body itself.

A Christian leader had developed some excellent material for church growth. A pastor asked if it were permissible for him to use the material in his church. The answer was, "Yes, this is not my material. It belongs to the church. The Lord gave it through me to build up His body. It is not mine. He only gave it through me."

The body is to call for the gifts of its members to be used. Members are responsible to the body in their use of gifts. What blessed potential! God has endowed the body with gifts sufficient to meet the needs of the church in doing "the work of the ministry, for the edifying of the body of Christ," (Eph. 4:12).

Gifts are distributed through the individual member. Each member has the privilege and responsibility of utilizing those gifts. Members have the option of whether or not they will be faithful to their Lord and church in utilizing the gifts God has given them.

What is being done with gifts by members? First, some are withholding gifts sinfully from our Lord and from His body. They are unfaithful servants. Like the man in our Lord's parable, they hide their talent in the earth.

Second, some are prostituting their gifts. They are selling them to the world. They are not using them for God. The world and the devil will pay for any gift God has given a person. They will pay in terms of prestige, power, position, and money.

A lay friend of mine has a gift of exhortation and evangelism. He was a university music professor. He designed and taught the first piano course ever to be done over television.

A secular company made him an attractive offer for his program and services. He could have made a fortune financially by marketing his gifts to the world. But this was not of God. God had another plan for him. Instead, the layman is utilizing his gifts in his local church as a volunteer. He is leading many people to Christ. He is using his gifts to equip many others to share Christ. No one but God knows how many people have come to know Christ because this layman refused to prostitute his gifts to the world.

The gifts laypersons use to glorify our Lord in the life of His church such as leadership, administration, teaching, and soul-winning could be used in the world in other ways. The time and ability required by a church finance committee chairperson or a department director could be spent in the business world to earn additional dollars. Satan constantly tempts God's people to prostitute the gifts God has given.

Third, some are in the process of discovering gifts. Every member of the church has at least one gift, probably more. But many are like I was. I did not think I had any gift with which to serve God. Through the encouragement of the church and the work of His Holy Spirit, God taught me that He had endowed me with gifts. As I began to serve, gifts began to come to the surface. We need to challenge every member to discover the gifts God has given.

Fourth, some are developing the gifts they possess. They are beginning to exercise their gifts. They are growing. Church leaders can do no better thing than to assist each member in discovering and developing the gifts God has given to him or her.

Fifth, many are utilizing their gifts to build up the body of Christ and glorify Him. A church can never function with a "hired staff" mentality. It will become effective as the leaders use their gifts to equip others for the work of the ministry. The total involvement of lay members of the church in ministry is the key to great power and growth within the church.

The promise of God to the church is: "My God shall supply all your need according to his riches in glory by Christ Jesus" (Phil. 4:19). Gifts come from God to bring glory to His Son and to make His child a fruitful Christian. As gifts are used, every need is met, both of the church body and each individual.[5]

Jesus is the Head of the church, His body, that in all things He might have the preeminence (see Col. 1:18).

Questions

1. Using the analogy of the human body, explain how the body of Christ, the church, can have diversity of members, yet be united.

2. How do you see yourself fitting into the body of Christ that is your local church? What part of the body are you?

3. What are some things your church can do to improve the balance of unity and diversity in worship?

2 Exalt the Savior:

Through Building the Fellowship

And these things write we unto you, that your joy may be full. This then is the message which we have heard of him, and declare unto you, that God is light, and in him is no darkness at all. If we say that we have fellowship with him, and walk in darkness, we lie, and do not the truth: But if we walk in the light, as he is in the light, we have fellowship one with another, and the blood of Jesus Christ his Son cleanseth us from all sin (1 John 1:4-7).

Fellowship and Church Growth

Fellowship is one of the keys to the effectiveness of a church.[1] A church will never grow beyond its fellowship. If the fellowship is right, the church will continue to minister, witness in love, and be built up in maturity and in number. But if the fellowship is not right, the church will decline and eventually die. If the fellowship is right, the church can work through any problem and continue to grow. But if the fellowship is disrupted, everything else goes down. Attendance will drop. Giving will decrease. Outreach will stop! Building the fellowship of a local church is crucial to its growth.

The Meaning of Fellowship

What is fellowship? Why is it so important? The very word *fellowship* is one of euphony. It is a beautiful, flowing word. The Greek term *koinonia*, from which we get our

English word *fellowship*, is a household word today. The very saying of that word is a thing of beauty. It is the sharing together of a common life. It is the bond of love and unity that keeps God's people one.[2] Someone has said, "Fellowship is two fellows in one ship." It suggests a binding partnership.

Fellowship is more than handshaking, backslapping, friendly smiles, and warm welcomes, though it includes these. It is not just social gatherings—cookies and coffee after church. It is much more.

Fellowship is a tough kind of love. It comes to grips with the nitty-gritty, unpleasant, difficult things that tend to divide God's people. Fellowship is the determination to love one another and stay together. Fellowship refuses to allow wrong to divide. It is the key to real life in a church. A church will never go beyond its fellowship in its growth, outreach, ministry, or meaning for its members.

Two Aspects of Fellowship

Fellowship within any church is twofold: vertical and horizontal. First is our fellowship with God. Second is our fellowship with one another. Both of these are spoken of in 1 John 1:6-7.

Fellowship with God

First, as God's children we have fellowship with Him. Disobedience breaks our fellowship with God. When fellowship with God is broken, it is impossible to have a right fellowship with one another.

However, broken fellowship with God may be restored. First John 1:9 says, "If we confess our sins, he is faithful and just to forgive us our sins, and to cleanse us from all unrighteousness." It is then that our joy becomes full. When we walk in the light as He is in the light, we have fellowship with Him and with one another.

The way is set forth by our Lord for fellowship to be restored with Him. Three words in 1 John 1:9 give us God's way for restored fellowship.

First, the word *confess* comes from the Greek word *homologeo*: *homo*—"the same as or alike," *logeo*—"to speak or to say a word." Confess, then, means to say the same thing as or to agree with God about our sins. If we confess our sins, we identify them as God identifies them. We look upon our sins as God looks upon them.[3]

Human nature revolts against agreeing with God about our sins. Instead, we attempt to excuse our sins. We attempt to justify, rationalize, minimize, blame others, or compare our sins with those of others.

Instead of confessing a lie, human nature says, "Oh, it was just a little white lie." Instead of admitting that a thing is wrong, human nature simply says, "Everyone does it." Or, "It is someone else's fault." Victory can never come as long as sin is minimized. Confession of sin opens the life so that God can deal with it.

Keith Miller told the story of a salesman who had become a Christian.[4] The salesman had been padding his expense account. He charged his company with personal items. When he become a Christian, he continued to do the same thing. One night during his devotional time, God began to deal with him. He was reading and praying. As he attempted to pray, he could only think of the expense account. Finally, he realized that it was the expense account about which he was to pray.

He confessed that he had been stealing, that he was a thief, that he had been padding his expense account. It broke his heart! He agreed with God about his sin. He asked God to forgive him and cleanse him. He got off his knees with a sense of relief and release.

The next day when he was tempted to do the same thing again, he could not. All he could think of was the night before when God had dealt with him and he confessed to being a thief. God had forgiven and cleansed him. He could not do it again.

Second is the word *forgive*. It means or remit or erase. Forgiveness is illustrated by a cloud that floats overhead in the sky. It takes different forms and shapes. While we watch, it disperses and disappears before our eyes. The cloud is no longer there. Where did it go? It is no more. So it is with our sins, when God forgives.

God puts our sins as far from us as the east is from the west and remembers them against us no more. He puts them under the blood of Jesus so that He no longer sees our sins. They are forgiven.

Do you remember your sin? Do you think back about that terrible thing you did? But you confessed that sin to the Father! God has forgotten it. He remembers it against you no more. Leave it behind. Leave it with Him. Do not return to it in thought or act.

Satan would defeat you by bringing it to your mind again and again. God has forgiven it. Leave it behind. When we continue to dwell upon a thing in our mind, it remains fresh and vivid to us.

At one time my family lived near downtown. I knew every store, every house on the street. But we moved away. Now I could not tell you what color the houses are or which stores are there. I do not go by there anymore. Just so with our sins. We need to quit going by there. It will grow more and more vague in your mind and your heart when you quit going by.

Third, God cleanses us from sin. *Cleanse* is the Greek word *katharizo*.[5] From it we have two English words *catheterize* and *catharsis*, one a medical term and the other a psychological term. To catheterize is to remove the impurities from a human body. Catharsis means the release of pent-up and damaging emotions.

When we confess our sins to the Father, He spiritually catheterizes us. He removes the poison of sin from our life, and we are cleansed. On the basis of that cleansing, fellowship with God is restored. Then we can have fellowship one with another in a meaningful way.

Fellowship with One Another

One of the first signs of backsliding is the tendency to draw away from one another. When we are having fellowship with God in truth, we will also have intimate and meaningful fellowship with one another. This is true in our homes, in our community, and in our church.

When Jesus Christ is exalted, He is first in each of our lives. Christ is not divided. He brings us together in oneness of fellowship. What a blessed and beautiful thing! We can never be up on Jesus and down on one another at the same time.

Two Types of Fellowship

Exclusive Fellowship

In our world and in some churches, two types of fellowship may be seen. The first is *exclusive* fellowship. Have you ever been excluded? In this kind of fellowship, you come into a room and sit down in the circle of people. But you realize that just as surely as if you were outside in the hall, you are not "in." Being excluded is painful. Carl Sandburg once said that the harshest word in the English language is the word *excluded.*

Civic or social clubs may draw their circles of exclusiveness. Worldly organizations may exclude others. But in church, there is no place for such an attitude. Unconsciously, an attitude of exclusiveness can develop in a church or in a church group. The very thing that makes our church meaningful can unconsciously develop an exclusiveness of others. We can begin to enjoy one another so much that we become insensitive to the outsider who comes into our midst.

This happened in the case of a young couple who visited

our Sunday School. They had visited the church. They were considering becoming members. But after visiting the Sunday School class they did not come back. They indicated that they were going to seek another church.

As pastor, I asked them why they had come to that conclusion. They indicated that they did not feel that they were a part of the Sunday School class. They had visited the Sunday School on the Sunday before Christmas. The young adult class was excited about visiting their families for Christmastime. All of the young couples had attended the early morning worship service. They were so excited about their own activities that they were insensitive to the new couple. When Sunday School was over, they quickly left to be on their way to Mom's house for Sunday dinner. The new couple was left behind to find their way into the church service and sit alone.

What should have happened in that situation? Someone should have taken a personal interest in the new couple. They should have remained at the end of Sunday School to escort them into the worship service. They should have stayed for the worship service and sat with them, even if it meant going to church twice on Sunday morning.

Any church that reaches people must develop a fellowship that is sensitive to the needs of others. In defense of the Sunday School class, the new couple did have an attitude of expecting rejection. Anytime persons expect rejection, they usually find it. However, our fellowship needs to be so sensitive to others that we discern that attitude. We must take the initiative to break down barriers and reach through to meet the needs of those who are withdrawn and negative.

Barnabas is the person in the New Testament who demonstrates that kind of discerning, unselfish spirit.[6] Paul had been excluded by the disciples in Jerusalem. Barnabas took Paul under his wing. He nurtured him. He stood up for him. He brought him into the fellowship. How tragic it would have been had the cause of Christ missed Paul. Barnabas is to be commended and congratulated. Our churches need to be full of Barnabas kinds of people.

Inclusive Fellowship

The second kind of fellowship—and the kind that belongs in our Lord's church—is *inclusive.* Jesus' commission is inclusive of all who will respond to His invitation. With His warmth of love we are to reach out to people of all kinds. Regardless of their social, racial, economic, political status, we are to be sensitive to their needs.

First John 2:2 is an inclusive verse. "And he is the propitiation for our sins: and not for ours only, but also for the sins of the whole world." John 3:16 is inclusive. Matthew 28:18-20, the Great Commission, is inclusive, as is 1 John 2:9, "He that saith he is in the light, and hateth his brother, is in darkness even until now."

An inclusive fellowship attracts people. Out in the world it is dog-eat-dog, backbiting, and back stabbing. The church should be an island of love in a sea of hatred and competition.

Glory of Fellowship—The most beautiful thing in this earth is the radiant, Christ-filled body of a church living within a community, permeating that community with the Christ-life. No one person can fully express the life of Jesus. The collective body of Christ possesses all His qualities. As we come together in unity, lifting up Jesus as Head of the church, His personality fills the body. He draws every member into a closeness of fellowship that demonstrates His personhood and love.

A church like this, indeed, becomes the salt of the earth and the light of the world. It penetrates every strata of its community. It penetrates the social, moral, political, economic, and spiritual realms of a community to make the Christ-life real. The church becomes a transforming agent for righteousness. This is the type of fellowship seen in the New Testament church in the Book of Acts.

Organized for Fellowship—A church should organize it-self to build the fellowship within. The Sunday School is a natural organization within the life of the church where this can happen. In fact, every church organization can con-tribute meaningfully to fellowship building.

Threats to Fellowship

Satan is not pleased when a church has a great fellow-ship. He will do anything he can to disrupt it. The church in Acts was experiencing great fellowship. There was tremen-dous numerical growth and victory. Then Satan began to attack.

In Acts, chapters 4, 5, and 6, three attempts of Satan to disrupt the fellowship of the church are seen. Satan's strate-gies have not changed. He still uses the same tactics.

External Opposition

Tho Sadducees and religious leaders launched an attack on the church. They threatened the church. They charged the church to speak no more to anyone in the name of Jesus.

What was the response of the church? Did they elect a committee to go to city hall to appeal for their rights of reli-gious liberty? Did they circulate a petition to send to the governor? No! They appealed to a Higher Authority. They got on their knees before God in prayer. They used the greatest weapon available to all humanity.

What did they pray? Did they ask God to give them safe-ty? Did they ask God to lift the persecution? Did they ask God to remove the pressure of external opposition? No! They prayed for boldness to speak the Word of God regard-less. They prayed for boldness to preach and witness even if they were killed for doing so. They prayed for courage, if need be, to die with the Word of Jesus on their lips.

This was victory! The pressure of external opposition served to solidify the fellowship of the church. With greater enthusiasm and power, they preached and taught in the name of our Lord.[7] When the fellowship stays true, external opposition serves to strengthen. It binds the people of God closer to one another and closer to God.

Critics are always attacking the Lord's church. We need to learn God's way of facing the world's critics. A church should never base its policies on its critics. The policies of the church need to come from God. The church needs to stop playing "footsie" with the world. While we must be sensitive to people, the church is to please God.

The church must not be like some politicians who run for office. They keep their finger on the pulse of public opinion. They take public-opinion polls. Then they say what they *think* people want to hear. God helps us to be the church the world needs rather than the church the world demands.

Our possibility of overcoming Satan's attack of external opposition is not in our knowledge of the world. It is not in our psychology. It is not in our own strategy. It is in the Lord Himself.

Revelation 12:10-11 says,

> For the accuser of our brethren is cast down, which accused them before our God day and night. And they overcame him by the blood of the Lamb, and by the word of their testimony; and they loved not their lives unto death.

We can overcome, first, through the power of the blood of Jesus. They claimed the power of the blood. They looked to Jesus who died for their sins and had already won the victory over Satan on the cross. His blood has almighty power. Satan was defeated at the cross. We must claim the finished work of Jesus on the cross.

Second, Satan is overcome through bold testimony. When we become timid about our testimony for Jesus, Satan gets the edge.

A once successful businessman nearly destroyed himself drinking alcoholic beverages. Then God touched his life. Clifford said, "I had a turnaround at that moment." He quit drinking that day! That hour! That moment! He began walking with God. He served God. He was in church every time the doors were open. He began to witness for the Lord Jesus.

Years later, I asked him, "Clifford, are you still living for God?"

He said, "I surely am." There was joy in his voice.

I asked him, "How do you do it? How do you stay faithful?"

He said, "I just keep giving my testimony for Jesus. I can't backslide while I'm giving testimony for Jesus."

"They overcame [Satan], . . . by the word of their testimony."

Third, "they loved not their lives unto death." They realized that their lives were expendable for Jesus. They were not out to save their own lives. They were ready to lose their lives for Jesus' sake. They were faithful even unto death.

An attitude of self-protection gives Satan the upper hand. When our lives are placed in the hand of Jesus, when we become obedient to Him no matter what, Satan cannot touch that life. That is victory!

Satan's attempt to overpower the church and disrupt its fellowship through external opposition failed. But what could he not do through external opposition, he attempted in another way.

Invasion of Hypocrisy

He decided to infiltrate the church with insincere people. This would water down the fellowship of that power-filled church.[8]

Ananias and Sapphira observed what was happening in the church. They saw people receiving attention and joy through selling their property and bringing the proceeds into the treasury of the church. They sold their possessions but kept back part of it instead of bringing all of it as did the others. They attempted to appear to be what they were not.

They wanted to appear to be notable and sacrificial Christians. They wanted to appear to be totally committed. But they were not. That sort of compromising member waters down the fellowship of the church. It minimizes the power and effectiveness of the church.

But God protected the fellowship. Hypocrisy in a fellowship of true believers sticks out like a sore thumb. Peter detected it. He confronted it. God dealt with them. God smote them. They died! Right on the spot. And they carried them out (Acts 5:1-10).

It would be better to be cast into a den of hungry lions than to become an instrument of Satan to invade a Spirit-filled fellowship of an obedient church. It is a dangerous thing to become Satan's instrument in disrupting a fellowship. God will protect such a fellowship.

Internal Dissension

In Acts 6, what Satan could not accomplish by external opposition and by the invasion of hypocrisy, he did temporarily through internal dissension. This is the most effective tool of Satan in destroying a church fellowship.

How does such a thing happen? Verse 1 says, "In those days, when the number of disciples was multiplied, there arose a murmuring of the Grecians against the Hebrews, because their widows were neglected in the daily ministration." It happened at a time when the number of disciples had multiplied greatly. Great and rapid growth is desirable but dangerous. There was rising tension of spiritual immaturity. They faced the challenge of a heterogeneous membership and need of organization. There were the local people and the outsiders. People who were in Jerusalem from other countries came into the church.

The outsiders accused the apostles of neglecting them in the daily ministration. Whether the people were actually neglected, or simply felt neglected, is immaterial. The results were the same. The response was: "there arose a murmuring."

Visualize what was happening. Upon the calm sea of the life of the church, there came ripples. The ripples became waves! The waves became a storm that would all but sink the ship of the church!

Spiritual growth declined. Soul-winning stopped. Outreach dropped sharply. There was turmoil. The fellowship was disrupted through murmuring. The word *murmur* is an onomatopoeia.[9] It is a word that sounds like what was happening. The Greek word for murmur is even more pronounced: *goggusmos*. It is a harsh, ugly, guttural word. Harshness and ugliness had flared up. They spread like wildfire. The only thing faster than the speed of light is the church grapevine!

What was the source? A group of little old ladies, the least likely group in the church. Who would ever think that the little old ladies in the church would be so used of the devil to disrupt the fellowship. But don't be surprised. Satan will use anyone who will let him. He will use little old ladies, little old men, little old young people, little old deacons, or the little old preacher! Satan will use any group of little people who will allow him to infiltrate the church with murmuring and dissension.

The progress of the church stopped! People were not being reached or grown in the Lord. The attention was turned inward upon the trouble of the church. A church cannot go forward when the fellowship is disrupted. A church has only so much energy, time, and gifts. If these are consumed on internal strife and negativism, there will be none left for ministry and witness.

A pastor whose church was having conflict said, "I've not had time to witness to the lost, prepare any messages well, or to minister to those in need. I am being consumed by the time it is taking to deal with the strife in the church."

How was internal dissension resolved in the New Testament church? The apostles were the key. They were mature leaders. They acted instead of reacting.

The mark of maturity is to tackle the problem rather than attacking the people. The apostles could have attacked the women. They could have said, "You sorry old ladies! After all we've done for you, you do not appreciate it. You're not submitting to pastoral authority. You are attacking us and murmuring. You must leave the church."

The apostles did not react. They acted in righteousness. They dealt with the problem. They said, "We have more to do than we can get done. There are needs here that we cannot meet. We need help."

They did not take the criticism personally. They asked the church to seek out seven men who could be assigned responsibility for meeting these needs. We believe that these seven men are the prototypes of the New Testament deacon. They were to be men who were full of faith, full of the Holy Spirit, and full of wisdom. They were to be men who had the confidence of the people. They were to meet specific needs. But their primary responsibility was to heal the fellowship.

When the need was met, the problem was resolved. Wise deacons and pastors give attention to healing the fellowship. When the fellowship of the church was healed, the ministry became effective again. There was joy. There was excitement and enthusiasm. There was effective evangelism. Good deacons are helpers, healers, and harvesters.

The result of restored fellowship was threefold. The Word of God increased, the number of disciples multiplied greatly, and a great number of the priests were saved (v. 7). When the fellowship got right, the church became stronger in evangelism. Even the hard cases began to get saved. This will be true in the life of any church. When the fellowship is right, the church will reach people with power.

Satan failed in his attempt to destroy the fellowship of the New Testament church. As we lift up Jesus as Head of the church, we too can overcome Satan to keep the fellowship strong.

Basis of Fellowship—Balanced Church Life

Another principle in building a great fellowship is a balanced church life. There is a perpetual tendency in the life of any church to move off into tangents. A church limits itself if its emphasis and ministry appeal to only one segment of its community. It also limits itself if it emphasizes only one or a few select ministries. For a church to reach its full potential it must have balanced emphases and balanced programs. Dr. David Womack in his book *The Pyramid Principle* suggests that a church's growth may be compared to building a pyramid.[10] A pyramid is constructed first by building the base. Then the pyramid is built up to its apex. The pyramid will collapse if its structure expands beyond the base support. Just so, a church cannot grow greater than its base support.

A fourfold emphasis is needed for balance in the church life. The emphasis must be Christ centered, person centered, Bible centered, and obedience centered.

Build Balanced Emphases

Christ Centered—First, the emphasis of a dynamic fellowship is Christ centered. Colossians 3:23 says, "Whatsoever ye do, do it heartily, as to the Lord, and not unto men." Here is a great motto by which to live. Here is the basis of true enthusiasm. Constant stress on keeping every activity geared toward bringing glory to Jesus is the priority.

Christ centeredness is subjective. How can it be maintained? This is difficult to say. But, surely, if we do not continue to emphasize that every activity and event must be Christ centered, soon it will not be. Every program, activity, and meeting should be put to the test of being Christ centered.

Person Centered—Second, every program and ministry of

the church must be person centered. Other approaches may be taken, but they do not build a strong fellowship.

A number-centered approach will not build an effective fellowship. Numbers are important, but only as they represent persons. Numbers for their own sake are out of place in the life of a church. Numbers are important. Biblically, we see much of numbers. In Acts 2 about three thousand souls were added to the church in one day. We know because somebody counted them. It is an exciting thing to read Luke's reporting of the numbers. Jesus fed five thousand men besides the women and children. Somebody counted, and John reported. The numbers are important because they represent persons. Jesus is person centered.

We must not be dollar centered. Some see church people as dollars to be gained. In one church, a leader was overheard to indicate that more people needed to be reached in order to have greater giving, so the building payment might be met. Our world is dollar centered. This has no place in church.

When I was in college, I met a young insurance salesman. He was working his way through college. One day as we had coffee he shared with me that every person he met meant five dollars to him. He had calculated just how many people he needed to meet in order to make a sale. Then he calculated that each person he met would mean five dollars to his income. Immediately the red flag went up in my mind. I asked, "How much do I mean to you?" I found out—just about five dollars.

An effective church cannot become building centered. Some make buildings primary. Buildings are to be used to minister to people.

One church was asked by a director of missions to allow some of their rooms to be used to minister to a poor ethnic group. They refused! They said, "We do not want that kind of people in our building. They will ruin our building." A church needs to be a good steward. Buildings must be maintained properly and respected. But buildings are for ministry to people.

A church should not be program centered. Programs are used for people, not people for programs. Some churches reverse the principle. They establish programs and expect people to fit them. We need to tailor our programs to meet the needs of people.

People are primary. We need to see people not as flat-surface pictures, things to be used, objects to be manipulated, numbers to be counted, nor dollars to be gained. We need to see people as the object of Jesus' love. We need to love people. We need to listen to people. We must give ourselves, as a church, to meet the needs of people. Jesus came for people.

Bible Centered—Third, it must be Bible-centered fellowship. Second Timothy 3:16-17 says,

> All scripture is given by inspiration of God, and is profitable for doctrine, for reproof, for correction, for instruction in righteousness: That the man of God may be perfect, thoroughly furnished unto all good works.

The Bible is the Creator's manual for successful living. If I purchase a new automobile, I will read the owner's manual. It was published by the people who built the car. They are qualified to tell me how to maintain and operate it effectively and efficiently. They designed and manufactured it. If I am smart, I'll pay attention to what they say.

The Creator is capable of guiding us into successful living. He has given us His guidebook. The Bible is His manual for successful living. Keep the fellowship Bible centered.

Obedience Centered—Fourth, a balanced emphasis in the fellowship must be obedience centered. James 1:22 instructs us, "Be ye doers of the word, and not hearers only, deceiving your own selves." A strong fellowship will be committed to obey every command discovered in the Scripture.

In a church near an Air Force base, a young sergeant was

saved. A month later, he came to his pastor to tell that he had a real problem. The sergeant said, "When I was saved, I made the commitment to obey whatever command from God I discovered in the Bible. My problem is that I've read that I'm to tithe. I do not have the money. I do not have enough to live on now without tithing. What shall I do?"

As his pastor I replied, "I certainly sympathize with you. The only way I have ever been able to tithe has been to bring the first tenth to God. Then, let the other nine tenths go as far as it will. My family and I have learned that we can live better on nine tenths obeying God than on ten tenths living in disobedience."

The sergeant reflected a deep faith when he said, "I'll do it and trust God." About three months later, the sergeant said that after beginning to tithe, he found he was doing better financially than he ever had.

Let every class and let every group in the church commit to obey whatever command from God that is discovered in His Word. Search the Scriptures to find what God commands. Claim His promises. What God commands, we can do. It will intensify the greatness of the fellowship of the church.

Build a Balanced Program

A growing church will build a balanced program for all ages and types of people. Five things are keys.

A Powerful Worship Service—This includes a warm spiritual climate of prayer. A heartfelt worship experience in singing. Spirit-anointed preaching from God's Word.

A Solid Education Program—Quality education provides powerful biblical teaching and nurturing on a small-group basis. The education program must complement a powerful worship service. Every person needs the intimacy of a small-group fellowship in nurture of his life.

A Dynamic Evangelism Thrust—Effective evangelism consistently, daily, reaches people for Christ. No greater joy is experienced in the life of a Christian than in bringing another to know Jesus. New converts coming into the fellowship bring a freshness that gives continuing vitality.

A Consistent Program of Pastoral Care and Nurture— Spiritual nurture must be provided for every member. Counseling and guidance is a must. Many churches can reach more people than they can effectively care for in pastoral ministry. It is important to develop a program of pastoral care that incorporates new members into the body of Christ.

A United and Growing Fellowship—As all members give themselves to build that great fellowship by lifting up Jesus, multitudes will be drawn to Christ and the church.

Careful attention must be given to building balanced emphases and programs in the fellowship of the church.

Questions

1. Satan threatens the fellowship of a church through external opposition, invasion of hypocrisy, and internal dissension. To what degree can a church have genuine fellowship if Satan is successful with any of his threats?

2. What are examples of an inclusive fellowship in your church?

3. What are examples of an exclusive fellowship in your church? How can you improve the inclusive fellowship?

3 Exalt the Savior:

Through Building the Fellowship— Pastor and People

Fellowship does not just happen. It must be built and maintained. Who builds the fellowship of a church? Three groups within the church are fellowship builders. The pastor and pastoral staff, the deacons, and the total church body. All must work together to build an effective fellowship in the church.

Pastor and Pastoral Staff
(Acts 20:28; 1 Pet. 5:1-4; 1 Thess. 5:11-13; 1 Tim. 5:19)

A church has a shepherding ministry to its people and community. The church must nurture, spiritually feed, and minister to a total community. The church is to pour out its life to reach and save its community.

The pastor and staff give leadership to the church's shepherding ministry. The role of the pastor is meaningfully observed in Acts 20:17-38. Here, three words are used interchangeably for the office of the pastor. These words describe the function of the pastor.

Three Functions of the Pastor

Pastor *(poimen).*—The meaning is to shepherd, nurture, feed, and care for. The pastor and staff are to give spiritual nurture to the family of God. He is responsible to feed the church of God according to verse 28.

Bishop *(episkopos).*—The meaning is to oversee, superintend, administer. The pastor is to give oversight to the work of the Lord through the local church. This is a biblical assignment to the pastor. He may categorize some of the ministry of overseeing and delegate it to others. But he is responsible for the administrative life of the church.

Some pastors are uncomfortable with this aspect of ministry. Some have said that they want nothing to do with administration. They want only to preach the gospel. This is understandable. However, the preaching, feeding, nurturing ministry of the church is intermingled with administration. The church must be guided with a vision. Decisions must be made. If the pastor does not accept the responsibility of leadership, no one else can do it effectively. If the pastor does not lead, the church will flounder. The people will not follow another.

A pastor must be careful not to be consumed by administration. Staff and lay leadership must assist. But the pastor must accept responsibility.

Elder (*presbuteros*).—An elder is one who either by a proven life of wisdom or because of age has gained a place of respect and influence,[1] a leader by example. In this respect, the pastor is a model for the people. He leads by example.

The pattern of pastoral ministry is servant leadership. The pastor is a servant leader. Often he places himself under those he is leading to teach, instruct, encourage, motivate, and inspire. But the pastor must lead.

Two Dangers in Leadership

There are two dangers in leadership. The pastor may be an extremist in one of two directions. The children's game, "Follow the leader," is a good example. "Follow the leader" goes well if the leader is sensitive to the followers. If he is too daring, he attempts things that will discourage the followers. They soon drop out, and the game is ruined. On the other hand, if he is too cautious, the game becomes boring. The followers lose their sense of challenge and quit.

The pastor must be sensitive to his people. He must begin

with them where they are and lead them as they have the capability of following.

The pastor is a servant leader rather than an authoritarian, crack-the-whip kind of church boss. People can be effectively led but not driven. Let me illustrate by this suggestion. Imagine that you have laid a piece of rope on the floor. You desire to move the piece of rope across the room. How can it be done? You may take the far end of the piece of rope and begin to push it across the room. Of course, you will push it into one heap. It will not move across the room. If you desire to get the rope across the room, you must take it by the other end and gently draw it across the floor. People can be led but not pushed.

The ministry belongs to the church. The pastor is the servant of Christ to the people to equip them for their ministry. The pastor is a servant to servants of the Servant.

A multiple pastor/staff team is necessary as a church grows larger. In the New Testament church multiple pastors shared responsibility in leadership and ministry in the church. Acts 20:17-38 indicates that there were numerous pastors in the church at Ephesus. A pastoral staff team is one application of this New Testament pattern.

No one pastor can be everything that is needed in the church. As a church grows, additional staff support is needed. It has been my experience that one staff member is needed for every 150-200 people in attendance. These pastors may have various administrative assignments, but all assist the pastor in the nurturing and caring ministry.

Three Types of Staff Assignments

In our particular work, the pastoral staff has three types of assignments. The first are administrative assignments. Each pastoral staff member has them. Each supervises programs. Each has primary responsibility for such things as the music ministry, Christian education program, ministry

of evangelism, activities and recreation, various age-group
divisions, and so forth.

Second are pastoral assignments. Each pastor assists in
nurturing and caring for the needs of the flock. He is involved in membership visitation and encouragement, ministry to the sick, the needy, the bereaved, counseling, and so
forth.

Third are evangelistic assignments. Each pastor is to do
the work of an evangelist. Witnessing and soul-winning are
responsibilities of each pastor. Every staff member should
be a consistent life-style witness and a soul-winner. Each
should accept definite assignments for evangelistic visitation every week.

The overseeing pastor, sometimes called the senior pastor, is responsible for leadership of the staff team. Unity on
the staff is absolutely essential. These people must be, above
all things, for one another. Any dissension in the pastoral
staff team will be sensed through the church body. It will
create unrest and division.

The senior pastor may not supervise the entire staff. But
he must accept responsibility for the staff team spirit and
direction. For the church to grow, a pastor must be able to
share responsibility and rewards. A pastor will greatly limit
the way God can use him if he cannot delegate responsibility and rejoice in the success of those with whom he works.
It should be the goal of a pastor to assist every member of
the pastoral staff team in being a success.

For the church to continue to grow, laypeople must be
willing to accept the ministry of multiple pastors. Churches
that insist on the senior pastor visiting every sick person,
performing every wedding, or conducting every funeral cannot continue to grow. One pastor can only accomplish a certain amount in ministry. For the ministry to be enlarged
and extended, the other pastors' ministry must be accepted.
The spirit of the staff and church should be needs centered,

rather than personality centered. The important thing is that the need is met, not who does it.

Building the fellowship is the primary responsibility of a pastoral staff team. As the pastor and team ministers within the body of Christ in an effective way, needs are met, and the fellowship is built strong.

Three Priorities of the Pastor

Some of the soundest counsel that could ever be given are these three things: First, preach the Word. There is nothing else to preach. Second, love people—even when they don't love you and when they are not lovable. Sometimes we are not lovable. Third, keep your eyes on Jesus. You will never be disappointed. Disappointment comes when we take our eyes off Jesus and fix them on others or on ourselves. Disappointment always leads to discouragement.

Two responsibilities exist when a preacher becomes discouraged. He can repent or quit. God cannot use a discouraged preacher. When discouragement comes, the preacher is finished.

Discouragement is sin—the sin of self-centeredness. When we become discouraged, it means that we have gotten our eyes on ourselves rather than on Jesus. When discouraged, we face three alternatives: repent of the sin of discouragement, resign and move on, or quit the ministry altogether. Keep your eyes on Jesus to guard against getting disappointed or discouraged.

Relationship of People to the Pastor
(1 Thess. 5:12-13; Heb. 13:17; 1 Tim. 5:17-19; 1 Pet. 5:1-3)

When I began writing the material for this book, I had not included a section on the relationship of people to the pastor. I taught a conference in a city in another part of the state. While there, I met individuals from five different churches where the fellowship was being ripped to shreds. In every case, the problem was the relationship of pastor and people. I came to realize that this is one of the most severe problems we face today.

Nevertheless, I hesitated to approach the subject. As I searched my heart, I discovered that it was my own personal pride. I found myself hesitating to teach the people how they are to relate to the pastor. I was afraid of what they would think about me. Then God dealt with me.

People need to know how they are to relate to their pastor. If the pastor does not teach them, who will? I made the decision not only to write the material, but to teach it to our people. I asked God to give me a spirit of humility in sharing with our people these significant truths.

The vitality of the fellowship of a church is largely determined by two relationships: one, the relationship of lay members to each other; two, the relationship of laypeople to their pastor.

The ministry of the laity and of the God-called pastor/leader are two teachings which affect the life and work of a local church. To disregard or to minimize either renders the church powerless.

If the ministry of the laity is ignored, the work of the church will not be done. It is God's plan for laypeople to do the work of the ministry to build up the body of Christ in number by outreach and in maturity by discipling.

Equally true, if the ministry of the God-called pastor/leader is minimized or ignored, the unity of the church will disintegrate. Chaos and confusion will result. The people will not be equipped, and the work of the church will not be done. God has chosen to equip and lead His people through the Word of God ministered to the people through God's called, appointed leader.

It is a relationship to a person. Members are to regard the pastor as a Christian brother. They are to apply the same biblical principles in their relationship to him as to another Christian.

It is a relationship to a position. First Thessalonians 5:12-13 says,

> We beseech you, brethren, to know them which labor among you, and are over you in the Lord, and admonish you; And to esteem them very highly in love for their work's sake.

The position of the pastor is a God-established, appointed, anointed position. It is one of four basic areas of God's delegated authority in the world.

The four are: first, in the family, parents are God's appointed leaders. Second, in the government, leaders are God's delegated authorities to establish and maintain social order. Third, in the church, the pastor is called of God and anointed for leadership. Fourth, in business, the employer is God's appointed leader to provide work and economic needs for persons.[2]

As in other areas of life, when the God-given authority is ignored or attacked, disorder, confusion, and defeat take place. Just so, when the position of the pastor comes under attack or is ignored, the church is disrupted, the fellowship broken, and the witness is powerless.

The position of the pastor is God called. Acts 20:28 says, "Take heed therefore unto yourselves, and to all the flock, over the which the Holy Ghost hath made you overseers."

According to this verse and many others, the Holy Spirit calls and places pastors where He will. The undershepherd of God's flock is chosen of God. Here are three things every person ought to know about pastors. One, they have a calling no one else has. Two, they have a responsibility no one else has (Heb. 13:7-17). Three, they have an accountability no one else has. The pastor is ultimately accountable to God. No preacher can please everyone. No preacher should try. The preacher's aim should be to please God. The following humorous description of an ideal preacher made the circle of church papers a few years ago. I am unaware of its origin.

The Ideal Preacher

After hundreds of fruitless years, a model minister has been found to suit everyone. It is guaranteed that he will please all the people in any church.

He preaches only 20 minutes, but thoroughly expounds the Word.

He condemns sin, but never hurts anyone's feelings.

He works from 8:00 to 10:00 p.m. doing every type work from preaching in the pulpit to janitor work.

He makes $100 a week, wears good clothes, buys good books regularly, has a nice family, drives a nice car, and gives $50 a week to the church.

He stands ready to give to any good cause, also.

His family is completely model in deportment, dress and attitude.

He is 26 years old and has been preaching for 30 years.

He is tall, short, thin, heavyset, handsome, has one brown eye and one blue eye, hair parted in the middle, left side dark and straight, right side blond and wavy.

He has a burning desire to work with teenagers and spend all his time with the older people.

He smiles all the time with a straight face because he has a sense of humor that keeps him seriously dedicated to his work.

He makes 15 calls a day on church members, spends all his time evangelizing the unchurched, and is never out of the office.

The pastor's position is one of God's delegated authority.[3] In the Old Testament and in the New, God appointed leaders to lead His people according to God's direction and vision. When the people followed the leadership of God's appointed leader, things went well. When the people rejected the leadership of God's appointed leader, God said they had rejected His leadership. First Samuel 8:7: "They have not rejected thee, but they rejected me."

The position of the pastor is not to be restricted by members of the body. When members place restrictions on God's appointed leader, they interfere with God's direction of his life and ministry. When they attempt to tell him what to preach, if he gives heed to them, he may miss the message God has for him to preach.

Second Timothy 4:3 tells one of the characteristics of the evil last days. People will get themselves preachers who will say what they want to hear rather than preach God's message.

The position of the pastor is not to be attacked by members of the body. Several injunctions from the Scriptures are given: 1 Timothy 5:1 says, "Rebuke not an elder, but entreat him as a father." Verse 19 says, "Against an elder receive not an accusation, but before two or three witnesses." Psalm 105:15 says, "Touch not mine anointed, and do my prophets no harm."

You may want to study several examples from Scripture: the case of Miriam (see Num. 12:1-10); the children of Israel (Num. 14); Korah, Dathan, and Abiram (see Num. 16); the Amalekite soldier (see 1 Sam. 31 and 2 Sam. 1); Elisha (see 2 Kings 2:23-24).

The case of David provides an excellent illustration of the regard we are to have toward that one who has been chosen by God for a particular position. David had an opportunity to kill Saul. Saul was filled with evil. He had sought to slay David. David was counseled by his associates to kill Saul. David did cut off a piece of Saul's clothing. His conscience was smitten for even that (see 1 Sam. 24:4-12). A second time David had opportunity to kill Saul. But he said that God would judge Saul (see 1 Sam. 26:8-11). David said, "The Lord forbid that I should stretch forth mine hand against the Lord's anointed" (v. 11).

The decline of church after church can be attributed to the attack of people against God's appointed leader. In one case, a lay leader in the church compared every pastor with the one he had so dearly loved. None met his expectations. He led in running off from the church pastor after pastor. The doors of the church finally closed. The man fell ill. His illness was severe, but unexplained as far as medical science was concerned. He never recovered. He was evidently under the judgment of God.

Any person who is tempted to become involved in such action should consider the severity of the consequences. No one can touch the Lord's anointed and escape the consequences (v. 11). Those who do always justify it on the basis that it was done for the good of Christ and His church. But it always results in harm to the church. Innocent people are always drawn into the practice and hurt. Those who are involved must live with the consequences of what they have done.

Does this mean, then, that the pastor has responsibility and accountability to no one? Of course the pastor is responsible and accountable to both God and the church. But the people of God need to take care about what they do when the preacher gets wrong. What can and should they do? Let me suggest the following.

First, stay right. Keep a right heart. Refuse to be embittered, involved in talebearing, slander, or gossip. Practice Ephesians 4:30-32.

Second, pray for him and try to restore him. Treat him as a brother according to Galatians 6:1-2.

Three, keep unity in the church (Eph. 4:2-3).

Four, commit the pastor to God's discipline and judgment. God knows how to and does discipline His erring preachers. God's Word gives the promise. 1 Cor. 9:27—They may become castaways. James 3:1—They come under God's judgment. First Samuel 26:8-11—David said that God would deal with Saul: God may "smite him," he may "die," or he may perish in "battle." David was saying, "He is God's servant, and God can deal with him in any way He chooses. I am not going to play God and touch him." This is also true for God's preachers today. God can deal with them any way He chooses. We need to be careful to leave such dealings to God.

Anytime a rupture in the relationship of the pastor and people takes place, the fellowship of the church will disintegrate. Both pastor and people must give attention to building a good relationship. This is one of the primary ingredients of building a great fellowship in the church.

Deacons Are Fellowship Builders

The second group of fellowship builders are deacons. In Acts 6, the first deacons were set apart for the purpose of healing the fellowship. The fellowship was severely threatened. Seven deacons were appointed to meet the need that existed. As the need was met, the fellowship was healed.

Deacons have not been set apart to act as a board of directors. They were not ordained to run the church. They may receive any assignment the church delegates to them, but they are not a board to dictate to the church what it can and cannot do. Deacons are not to be watchdogs to ride herd on pastors.

Deacons assist the pastors in meeting the needs of the church of God. They free the pastors so that they can be more effective in the ministry of the Word and pastoring the flock. Let me suggest two approaches of deacon ministry in fellowship building. One is the deacon family ministry or deacon flock plan. The second is a deacon task force ministry.[4]

In the Deacon Flock Ministry, the church membership is divided into groups of families. Each group of families is assigned to a deacon for periodic contact and ministry. This plan offers a tremendous potential for fellowship building. The deacon and his wife make periodic visits to each of the homes of his flock. And another layperson can be assigned as a helper to the deacon.[5] We have called the lay helper a yokefellow.

Periodically, the deacon may meet with his flock for prayer meetings, social gatherings, Bible studies, and other activities. One way of doing this is a churchwide dinner. All the church family comes together. The families sit with their particular deacon. The pastor may share about the ministry of the church. An inspirational speaker may challenge the entire church fellowship. An annual Deacon Flock Banquet can be a tremendous fellowship builder.

A second approach is the Deacon Task Force Ministry. As the church membership is surveyed and various needs discovered, groups of deacons called Task Forces are assigned to meet those needs. This is a flexible approach toward the deacon ministry. It recognizes the differing gifts of each of the deacons. It also guarantees that the ministries of other organizations within the church are not duplicated by the deacons.

At various times we have used the following Task Forces: New Member Follow-up, Prospect Visitation, Absentee Member Visitation, Crisis Ministry, Homebound, Nursing Home Ministry, Bus Ministry, Hospital Visitation, and so forth. As deacons actively serve in the life of the church to minister to people, the fellowship of the church is made strong.

Every Member—a Fellowship Builder

In one sense, every member is a pastor. Someone looks to each member for spiritual nurture and guidance. It may be a child in the family. It may be a neighbor. It may be a Christian. Every member has a pastoral ministry.

As the membership of the church becomes sensitive to people, they begin to reach out to others to include them into the fellowship. Out in the community, each member extends the fellowship of the church as he ministers to those about him. When the church meets, every member reaches out in fellowship and ministry. When members arrive at the church for a meeting, they look for people whom they can assist. They greet people. They assist people in finding their way to classes and group meetings. They take personal responsibility in extending the fellowship of the church to others.

In such a church an atmosphere of love and warmth creates joy and enthusiasm. Pastor, deacons, and every member work together to build the fellowship of a great church.

Discipline of the Fellowship

The analogy of a human body has been used as an illustration for a local church. For a person to have a healthy body, discipline is necessary. Likewise, for a local church to be a healthy body of Christ, discipline is essential.[6]

A person with an undisciplined appetite will become obese. As a young preacher, I spent as much time as I could with older preachers. I wanted to learn everything I could from these who had had experience in the service of the Lord. I accompanied a fine pastor-evangelist to the revival meeting he was preaching. We were invited for dinner to the home of one of the church members. We sat down to a beautiful table laden with food. The older preacher jokingly remarked to me, "Darrell, having surrendered to preach as young as you have, by the time you are thirty years old you will weigh three-hundred pounds."

Surely enough, with that kind of food and the appetite I have, that would have been true. I would have been a five-foot-seven, three-hundred-pound freak rolling along instead of walking, except for one thing: discipline—discipline of appetite and exercise.

The same is true with the church. If a church goes on without discipline, it grows in out-of-proportion kinds of ways. It becomes a spiritual freak.

Three types of discipline are taught in the Scripture—formative, restorative, and amputative. At various times, a church must exercise each of the three in order to remain a healthy body of Christ.

Formative Discipline (Heb. 10:23-25)

Formative discipline is the normal attention that must be given to Christians in a growing body. It is spoken of in Hebrews 10:23-25:

> Let us hold fast the profession of our faith without wavering; (for he is faithful that promised;) And let us consider one another to provoke unto love and to good works: Not forsaking the assembling of ourselves together, as the manner of some is; but exhorting one another: and so much the more, as ye see the day approaching.

Formative discipline keeps the body growing, alive, and vital so that other forms of discipline are not necessary. God's people continue to encourage one another. They "provoke" one another to love and good works.

Every Christian at one time or another needs to be prodded along—to be provoked to love and good works. Colossians 3:16 charges the people of God to admonish one another.

Many times members stumble, faltering along so that they could not go on if other Christians did not reach out to extend a helping hand. We are members one of another. We are to encourage one another.

Restorative Discipline (1 Thess. 3:14-15; Gal. 6:1-2; Matt. 5:23-24; 18:15)

One of the first indications of backsliding is to withdraw from the fellowship of believers. When a believer begins to become slack in church attendance, something negative is happening.

Nurture, strength, and support are received through the body of the church. To withdraw from the fellowship in attendance isolates one from nurture and support. Soon other manifestations of sinful behavior appear. Spiritual diseases overcome the person.

The diseased member of the body needs attention.

Brethren, if a man be overtaken in a fault, ye which are spiritual, restore such an one in the spirit of meekness; considering thyself, lest thou also be tempted. Bear ye one another's burdens, and so fulfill the law of Christ (Gal. 6:1-2).

What is often done when a member becomes spiritually diseased and backslides? Nothing! He is often ignored, hoping that the problem or the person goes away. Sometimes he is attacked and condemned. He is kicked while he is down. Thus, he becomes more defeated.

Sometimes backsliders are rejected with hopes that they will leave without causing trouble.

At a conference one day, a pastor asked me about a family who had visited our church. They were members of his church. He asked if they had joined. He stated that he hoped they did join because his church did not need their kind.

I wondered what he thought about us. Then I began to examine myself.

I thought, *Is this the kind of attitude that I have toward people?*

I pray not. If a member has a problem, it is my problem. He may be critical, attacking, and difficult. But this simply indicates that the member has a need. It is my responsibility to minister to that member at the point of need. I am commanded to love him and bear his burden with him. I am to attempt to restore that member.

Why is restoration often not attempted? Very simply, it is because we do not care enough to pay the price and risk involvement. There is a risk in becoming involved with people who have problems. We must love them enough to take the risk of being hurt ourselves in order to restore them.

What should be done? Reclaim and restore. Discipline is necessary for spiritual growth. Our great example of discipline is Hebrews 12:5-11. God disciplines His children.

There is no child of the Father who does not receive discipline. His discipline is not for punishment but for profit. It is to heal, not to hurt.

Restorative discipline is necessary for the sake of the body. Otherwise, the body becomes a cripple when a member is overtaken with a fault. One member who becomes spiritually diseased and ailing ceases to be active and cripples the body.

Some years ago I was pastoring a new church. Since the church was just getting started, my salary was minimal. I received several invitations for evangelistic meetings. I was ashamed to wear the old shoes I had to the other church. I found a bargain table in the shoe department at one of the stores downtown. A brown, eight-dollar pair almost fit. They were just a little tight. I bought them.

By the time I had gone two weeks, one of them had worn a sore on my little toe. It became so painful I could hardly walk. I could not sleep at night. I wore house slippers into the pulpit. I doctored that toe and gave it careful attention in order to heal it.

Such an insignificant member as my little toe made my whole body sick. I did not even know I had it until it was sore. I did everything I could to bring healing to the toe. Every member of my body assisted. I was determined to restore that small, diseased member of my body. Just so, the church body must give attention to that one member to do everything possible to restore it. Otherwise, the whole body becomes a cripple because of one diseased member.

In the average church, there are so many spiritually diseased, backslidden members that the church is severely crippled. Much attention needs to be given to restoration. The average church can be illustrated by two concentric circles. The larger circle would be called the membership circle. It is made up of all those who have their names on the membership roll of the church. It includes many backslidden, spiritually diseased, peripheral members. The smaller circle within is the fellowship circle. It includes those who are living in intimate fellowship with the church. They are active in attendance and participation in the church life. They are committed to Christ.

The goal is for the fellowship to enlarge and extend until it includes all the membership circle. Restoration needs to take place until each member is included in the vital fellowship of the life of the church.

The attitude with which Christians should approach a ministry of restoration is given in Galatians 6:1. It is to be done in a spirit of meekness, humility, and love. We are to reach out to the brother or sister with a fault considering ourselves lest we also should be tempted. We must realize that whatever our fellow member does, we are capable of doing ourselves if we get our eyes off Jesus. We must be careful, realizing that attempting to restore a brother gives rise to temptation. We may be tempted toward sins of pride, self-righteousness, and judgmentalism.

Jesus outlines the steps to be taken in restoration (Matt. 5:23-24; 18:15-17). First, if you are the one offended, go to the person privately. Do not go to another first to enlist support. Go to the member personally and explain the fault between you and that person only.

If the member will not be reconciled, take two or three witnesses with you that every word may be established.

If the person refuses to hear them, tell it to the church.

If the person refuses to hear the church, let him be to you as a heathen. He has refused to hear the church. He has positioned himself in the place of an unbeliever. We are not to have intimate fellowship with the heathen. But we are to love and try to win the heathen to Jesus.

If another is offended at you, go to that person. Be reconciled to the person. Secure forgiveness.

Great power comes into the fellowship of the life of a church that will practice Jesus' principles of reconciliation and restoration. A fellowship of love refuses to give up. It continues to reach out to troubled brothers and sisters.

One example is an adult Christian man who became slack in his attendance to church. He drifted into worldly associations. He became involved in immoral relationships. Fellow members in his Sunday School department went to him in a spirit of love. They confronted him about his behavior. They dealt with him from the Word of God with hope. He came to repentance. He came before the church and asked for forgiveness. He was restored to the fellowship.

Another is the example of two young ladies who were involved in a conflict. They disagreed over a program involving one of the girls' organizations. One became convicted to ask forgiveness of the other. They were reconciled. They began a new working relationship that made the program successful.

In another case, a young man had been involved in immoral relationships. He was confronted by one of his Christian brothers in a spirit of love. When this failed, he was dealt with by the pastor and deacon officers. He came to repentance. He was restored to the fellowship. If action had not been taken to restore him, he would probably have left the church and embarrassed the cause of Christ.

If the steps Jesus has outlined are followed in the right spirit, restoration will usually be successful. However, when every effort for restoration has been rejected, the next step of discipline may be necessary.

Amputative Discipline (1 Cor. 5:4-7; Titus 3:10; 1 John 2:19-20)

Let us look again at the sore toe illustration. If the sore toe does not respond to treatment, rather than infect the rest of the body, it must be amputated. Just so, if the diseased member does not respond to treatment, the infection will spread through the rest of the body. Amputation may become necessary.

Sometimes, because of the severity of offense, a member

must be cut off from the body. This is not a pleasant thing to do. Amputation is always painful. Scripture gives five cases where amputation is necessary:

Immorality.—In 1 Corinthians 5:4-5, a member was guilty of flagrant immorality. It was infecting the rest of the body. Paul admonished that the member should be delivered to Satan for the destruction of the flesh that the spirit might be saved.

Heresy.—Titus 3:10 indicates that those who are guilty of heresy should after the first and second admonition be rejected.

False Professions.—First John 2:19-20 determines that those who go out from the church indicate that they were not a part of the church. After attempts to restore them, the church should let them go.

Rebellion Against Church Authority.—In Matthew 18:17, Jesus indicated that the person who refuses to hear the church should be considered as a heathen. The position taken is that of an unbeliever. The church should recognize the attitude and action of such a member. The church should consider this person as a nonbeliever.

Hypocrisy.—In this case, God purged the fellowship. In Acts 5, Ananias and Sapphira were smitten by the Lord. God purged the fellowship of the hypocritical members. This seems to be the case where tares were growing among the wheat. God brought His judgment to bear upon them.

How should amputated members be treated? First, the church should refuse to have intimate fellowship with them. In 2 Thessalonians 3:6-8, the apostle Paul instructed that we withdraw ourselves from every brother that walks disorderly and not after the tradition which he received of us. Second, the church should refuse to support the wrong living of the offender. "For even when we were with you, this we commanded you, that if any would not work, neither should he eat" (2 Thess. 3:10).

Third, the offending member should be refused an office

or place of leadership in the church. Fourth, he should be treated as Jesus instructed in Matthew 18:17, "as an heathen man and publican." How do we treat heathens and publicans? They are to be dealt with as unbelievers. We should seek to win them to Christ.

The purpose of amputation according to 1 Corinthians 5:6-7, first, is for the sake of the body. The influence of the offender will spread through the body like leaven. For the protection and purification of the church fellowship, offenders must be amputated.

Second, amputation should take place for the purpose of saving the offender. In 1 Corinthians 5:5, Paul's instruction was to deliver that person to Satan for the destruction of the flesh that his spirit might be saved. Perhaps he will be shocked to his senses. Second Corinthians 2:7 gives evidence that the discipline was successful. Apparently, the offender in the church of Corinth was restored through discipline.

If discipline is neglected, severe consequence follows. The member himself will become puffed up. He will be like the spoiled child who does not received guidance or discipline from his parents. He will begin to resent the church. The church that refuses to practice discipline will find its fellowship poisoned by the impurity that develops. The fellowship will be so weakened that the church will be paralyzed.

The life-force of the church is love. First Corinthians 13 is the best guide we have for building the fellowship of the church. Love is accepting. The God kind of love is unconditional. Love acts, giving itself to meet the needs of others regardless of return.

Much attention needs to be given to building the fellowship of the church. Be grateful for that fellowship. It cannot be found everywhere. In the world is strife and contention. Many churches have great inner turmoil. When the fellowship is right, be grateful for it.

Guard the fellowship by exalting the Lord Jesus Christ and striving to keep the unity of the Spirit in the bond of peace. By exercising discipline within the individual life and within the life of the church, guard the fellowship.

Grow it by loving one another, by working through problems. Grow the fellowship by carrying out Christ's commission and extending the fellowship to others.

When Jesus Christ our Lord is lifted up as the Head of the church, He draws together the members of the body into a unity that builds a beautiful and blessed fellowship.

Questions

1. If your church were an orchestra and your pastor the conductor, what kind of music would result?

2. What music would the lost person hear from your church?

3. How does your church delegate responsibility?

4. What can your church do to build fellowship?

4 Exalt the Savior:

Through Organization and Administration

Nothing is more finely organized than a healthy, functioning human body. Every part is joined together in such a way as to allow the whole body to function effectively and efficiently. Inside the head is the world's greatest computer. The brain instantaneously computes facts, coordinates all members simultaneously, and controls the entire body.

Christ is the Head of the church. He is the control center. He coordinates and controls the entire body. For a local church to function effectively, it must be properly organized and administered. If a human body loses its coordination, it will stumble and falter along. The same is true with the body of Christ. If church growth is to take place, there must be meaningful coordination and organization of members into unity in the body.

One of the New Testament words for the role of a pastor in the church is *bishop (episkopos),* meaning "overseer." This designates one of the pastoral responsibilities. The pastor is to take oversight of the church under the headship of the Lord Jesus, the Chief Shepherd (1 Pet. 5:1-4). This is the administrative responsibility of the pastor.

Administration—a Biblical Assignment (Eph. 4-15-16)

If administration is a biblical assignment to be cared for in the body of Christ, then it must be important. Organization and administration in the life of a church should not be relegated to the realm of insignificance. If a church is truly to lift up the Lord Jesus Christ and function effectively in our world, organization is a must.

Ephesians 4:16 suggests a meaningful coordination of every member in the body as one.

> The whole body fitly joined together and compacted by that which every joint supplieth, according to the effectual working in the measure of every part, maketh increase of the body unto the edifying of itself in love.

Two Keys to Church Growth

There are two keys to church growth under the headship and lordship of Jesus: spirit and organization.

Spirit

The spirit of a church is vital to its growth. A church can go nowhere if its spirit is not right. The fullness, work, and guidance of the Holy Spirit is essential for a local church to function effectively.

In the Scriptures Jesus is called the last Adam (1 Cor. 15:45-47). Going a step further, we would conclude that the church is the body of the last Adam, the Lord Jesus Christ. In Acts 2 the church was a lifeless body until the Holy Spirit came and filled it. The church was like the first man, Adam. God molded a physical body of clay. Adam lay motionless until God breathed into him the breath of life.

Before Pentecost, the church was a lifeless body. Then, God breathed into it His life. The church became a Spirit-filled, dynamic body of Christ. Without the Spirit, there is no life within the church. The Holy Spirit is primary.

Organization

What about organization? Some Christians seem to feel that the Holy Spirit is antiorganization. There was a time, as a young preacher, when I thought organization was anti-spiritual. I did not want to bother with organization. I thought that to really be spiritual the church needed simply to trust and obey the Lord. I did not realize that if we believe and obey God, we will build the church life according to biblical principles of organization and administration.

Organization Is Biblical.—Genesis 1:2 states that the Holy Spirit moved upon the face of the deep and brought order out of chaos. In an orderly, organized fashion God created the heavens and the earth and all that is within them (Gen. 1).

God's great leader, Moses, led the people of God out of Egyptian bondage into the wilderness. They bogged down and could not move forward. There were endless lines of people waiting to see Moses. Moses had to make every decision.

Moses' father-in-law Jethro—an outsider—observed the situation. He made a simple suggestion that was blessed by God. In Exodus 18:20-23, Jethro suggested that Moses organize the people into small groups with a leader over each group. Moses would lead the leaders. Moses would make the major decisions. He would delegate responsibility to his subordinate leaders.

Had Jethro not come along, the Israelites might still be in the wilderness. Many a church is in the wilderness of confusion because it ignored biblical principles of organization.

Jesus organized the multitudes in order to feed them in Mark 6:39-40. Paul set forth the need for organization in 1 Corinthians 14:33,40. He indicated that things should be done in an orderly way in the church of God.

In the early church, organization developed gradually to meet particular needs that arose. First, an apostle was elected to replace Judas (Acts 1:15-26). Then, seven deacons were selected to assist the apostles (6:1-7). Gradual development continued on through the Book of Acts.

Organization Is Necessary.—Organization is not primary, but it is necessary. Organization for organization's sake is wrong and defeating.[1] It should grow out of need. We organize to meet needs that arise. The ordination of the first deacons in Acts 6 is a fine example. A need arose. Men were selected and delegated with a responsibility of meeting that need. The result was the healing of the fellowship.

When organization is effective, the system itself is not apparent. Things simply get done without attention being called to the organization. People who look on and many who are involved may not realize why and how things are done. But because of effective organization, things have fallen into place.

An interesting and almost-amusing illustration of this very thing happened in our church. We were involved in a three-month Sunday School enrollment campaign. We called it "1000 New Members in 100 Days." We were about halfway through the program. A leading pastor in our state asked one of our key laypersons what particular organizational plan we were using. He asked if we were using a denominational program or some other.

Our layperson had been very involved in reaching people. But he had not been a part of the planning and organizational stage. He answered, "Oh, we are not using any organization plan at all. It is just happening." For all he knew, it was just happening. As pastor, I had given many hours to the planning process. Our educational director had given many more hours in putting together the organization. The department directors, teachers, group leaders, and others had spent time in organizing to make it effective. But as far as that particular layperson was concerned, there was no organization. It was just happening! That is exactly what he should have felt.

When the organization is out of kilter, it gets attention. Otherwise, things simply get done and those who are not involved in the organization do not realize that it is there.

When the organization is defective, things do not get done that should be. People become tense; they get disappointed;

they begin to blame one another. Then they blame the leader. The leader blames the people. They get the "blame game" going. Because of defective organization, the Spirit is grieved by the sinful behavior of such persons. The fellowship of the church is destroyed. The church declines.

Often, churches die for lack of effective organization. One particular church had a healthy Sunday School attendance of around four hundred. They called a pastor who did not believe in organization. He felt threatened when others were involved in decision making and planning. He set aside the organization. Things began to go undone. The pastor blamed the people. They all became discouraged. People began to leave. The church declined to the point where they were having only about fifty in Sunday School attendance.

Spirit and organization go hand in hand. I like to compare the church to a giant locomotive on a track. It has great ability to pull a heavy load. But it will not move an inch without power. The power is the Holy Spirit.

However, the locomotive will not move forward without wheels. Wheels represent the organization of the church. Like the wheels, organization gives the church mobility. It enables the church to move along and carry a great load for Christ.

Organization Is Natural.—Some are negative toward the organized church. They develop groups and call them non-denominational. In truth, "nondenominational" simply becomes the designation of their denomination.

Anytime any group comes together and does anything, two things happen. Leadership and organization emerge. Anytime three people get together, one of them will emerge as leader. A church needs to accept God's appointed leadership and follow sound organizational principles.

Personal Relationships Are Primary

While organization is necessary, it is not primary. The work of the Holy Spirit in the lives of people is primary. In all our programs we must remain people centered. Acceptance of persons and willingness to deal with problems should be our life-style. Otherwise, people will be alienated. In facing relationship problems, the church must be redemptive.[2]

We should follow the example of the apostles (Acts 6) in dealing with the problems. Attack the problem not the person.

The existence of a problem is evidence of an unmet need. God has committed Himself to His people to supply all their needs. In Philippians 4:19, we have God's promise: "But my God shall supply all your need according to his riches in glory by Christ Jesus."

Every problem is a divine opportunity for God to work. God permits a problem to arise that His own power and provision may be made manifest.

Attention to Details—Principles of Delegation

For any church program to be effective, attention must be given to details. Unattended details will kill a program. Careful organization must be used to cover every detail.

Don't leave loose ends dangling!
Don't never assume nothing!
Delegate each responsibility to a definite person.

1. Be specific.
   ● About *what* is to be done.
   ● About how to do it. If the "how" is important to you, make sure you specify that.
   ● About when it is to be done. Many leave a question mark about deadlines. Always communicate the deadline.

2. Put it in written form.
   ● For clarity of statement. Writing it will assist you in making sure you have stated it correctly.

- For understanding of the person responsible.
- For a record. If you are like most of us, you will tend to forget the exact details you have communicated. Both you and the person receiving your communication will need a record.

3. Confirm definitely the person's acceptance of responsibility. This may be done through a brief note, telephone call, or personal conference.

4. Establish checkpoints. Receive periodic progress reports for coordination and mutual support. Offer assistance along the way.

Delegating responsibility is a positive way of creating enthusiasm. It involves others in what is happening. It distributes the work load so that more can be done more effectively.

The simple procedures we have just outlined can save much confusion. What a frustrating thing it is to come to the time when a thing should have been done, but it has not! Have you had the frustrating experience of arriving at the time and place for an event to find that the sound system has not been set up? Everyone runs around like the proverbial chicken with its head cut off. There is confusion and embarrassment. Not only is this frustrating for the leader, but the people lose a measure of confidence in the leadership. Give attention to details.

People and Problems

Rejection and blame play a great part in the relationship problems of people. We need to love people, listen to people, and unconditionally accept them as persons even when their behavior is unacceptable (Eph 4:31-32).

Diagram 4.1

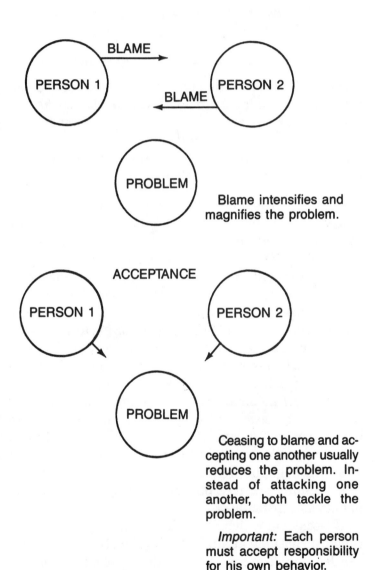

BLAME

PERSON 1

BLAME

PERSON 2

PROBLEM

Blame intensifies and magnifies the problem.

ACCEPTANCE

PERSON 1

PERSON 2

PROBLEM

Ceasing to blame and accepting one another usually reduces the problem. Instead of attacking one another, both tackle the problem.

Important: Each person must accept responsibility for his own behavior.

Many people have been conditioned to expect rejection. Their behavior is in response to the rejection they expect. Ceasing to blame and then accepting one another usually reduces the problem.

Problem-Solving Technique

One of the determining factors in the success of a person's life is in how he faces problems. One of the marks of a successful, secure person is that he faces problems in the right way.

A wise and successful Christian businessman said, "I do not see problems; I see challenges."

1. Identify the problem: state it simply. You have come a long way in resolving the problem if you simply identify it. Many people go about with a cloud of gloom over their heads. They have a real problem. But they never stop long enough to look at the problem, identify it, and seek the solution. They simply go on under the cloud of gloom.[3]

  a. Realize that every problem has a solution. All things are possible with God. There is no problem that is impossible. God has the right solution for every problem.

  b. Realize that every problem is an opportunity for God to work in your life and situation.

2. List all possible courses of action. There are at least three possibilities: positive, negative, and nothing. List the things you would consider doing. Also, list the things you would not want to do. List every *possible* course of action. This will help you in analyzing the problem.

3. Examine all possibilities in the light of biblical commands and principles.

4. Decide on which course of action to take. You may decide to do nothing at all. If that be true, then you have made the decision. You are on top of the problem rather than being under the gloom of this burden. At a given moment, the

wisest course of action to take may be to decide to do nothing at this time. With some problems, delayed action should be planned. Additional information may be needed. Your decision may be affected by the action of another person involved. You may set a time in the future by which to act.

5. Act: not to act is the equivalent of not deciding.

The problem-solving technique we have just discussed can be effectively used in your personal life, church, home, business, counseling, and in any personal relationships. I have used it many times in witnessing and soul-winning.

This was true in the case of a man named Joe. I was preaching in a meeting in Chicago. The pastor and I visited in Joe's home. Joe's wife was a new Christian who had just joined a Baptist church. Joe had a religious background but was not a Christian. He felt that he could not be active in church.

As we discussed his situation, Joe said, "I have a real problem." I asked Joe if we could identify his problem and see what he could do about it. Joe stated that he had been divorced and had remarried. For this reason he could not return to his former religion. The only way he could return would be to divorce his present wife. That was his problem about church.

I asked him if we could list his possible courses of action. Here's what he said: 1. "I could divorce my wife and return to my former religion. (But, I do not want to do that!) 2. I could do nothing. I could give no spiritual leadership to my family. Just sit at home. That is what I am doing now. 3. I could go with my wife to church."

I asked Joe if we could evaluate these three possibilities in the light of biblical principles. What is really right? Joe reasoned in the following way. "I know it is not the right thing for me to leave my wife and family. Besides that, I do not want to! I know it is not right for me to refuse to give spiritual leadership to my family. I really want to lead my family in the right way." "Is there any other alternative?" I asked. He replied, "Yes, I can go with my wife. I will do that."

Then, I explained to Joe how the church receives members on profession of faith in Jesus Christ. At that point, I shared with him God's plan of salvation. He prayed and committed his life to the Lord Jesus Christ.

This simple problem-solving technique may be used in a multitude of ways.

Making Meetings Meaningful

During a very busy day I received a phone call asking me to attend a three-o'clock meeting that afternoon. It was a very important meeting to the person who had called it. I did not feel that I had time to go, but I rearranged my schedule in order to have an hour to attend.

Nothing went right at the meeting. It began late. Poor preparation had been made. The meeting dragged on for an hour and a half, and it accomplished little. Finally, I had to leave.

I came back to my office realizing how important it is to make our meetings meaningful. This is a very important and often neglected area of the life of a church. Many meetings are held. But little attention has been given to how to make them meaningful.

Not only should a church leader know how to conduct meetings effectively, but he should train his people how to prepare for meetings, how to conduct them, and how to get the most out of them.

Here are some simple guidelines:

Primacy of Meetings

Meetings are essential for communication. They are necessary for planning and working together to carry out Christ's Commission.

Preparation for Meetings

1. Specify the objective of the meeting. Valuable time is wasted when the meeting's objective is unclear. Make yours a "meeting with a purpose."

2. Set a date of the meeting well ahead of time to avoid conflicts with other important events.

3. Establish a beginning and ending time for the meeting. You may say, "The meeting will be 7:00 to 8:00 p.m." This will allow participants to attend and plan other activities before and after. It will allow the person who has a crowded schedule to be able to attend without the possibility of spending an undetermined amount of time.

4. Notify ahead of time those who need to attend, so they can plan to attend without schedule conflicts. State the objectives, date, time, and place of the meeting.

5. Make thorough preparation for presentation and details for consideration during the meeting. Gather data, information, and materials necessary to make the meeting effective. Do not go to the meeting half prepared.

Pointers for Meetings

1. Begin on time; end on time.

2. Provide any supplies needed: note paper, pencils, chalkboard, projector, and so forth.

3. Keep the meeting positive. Deal with problems in a positive way. Participants should have the Spirit of Christ.

4. As much as possible, set up an agenda to guide the meeting.

5. Keep the meeting on course. Do not allow it to get sidetracked. At times, people will introduce unrelated subjects or will simply get on their favorite subject and try to monopolize the meeting with it.

The chairperson should say, "Excuse me, but that is another subject. Let's move on with the subject of the meeting.

If we have time at the end of the meeting, we will consider your subject."

6. Make sure accurate records are kept of the meeting.

7. Mail out minutes of the meeting to the committee. Make sure absentees receive necessary information.

8. Be sure to implement decisions made at the meeting as soon as possible.

Promotion of the Meeting

1. Do not be timid about promoting a meeting. If the meeting is necessary, it should be attended. Attendance failure will produce failure in the program the meeting is to support.

2. Notify those who are expected to participate in the meeting as soon as it has been set.

3. Send or call reminders a day or two before the meeting.

Personal Time Management

Time is the only real possession we have. It is granted to us by God Himself. We are responsible to Him for what we do with it. How we spend our time will determine the fruitfulness of our lives.

How we spend our time reveals what is truly god of our lives. If we spend several hours a day watching television, television is our god. If our time is spent in self-indulgence, self is our god. If we allow other people to control our time, they become our gods.

Often the statement is made: "I just do not have time."

The truth is: everyone has the same amount of time. Every person has twenty-four hours in every day. We decide what we will do with that time. A person gives time to that which he considers important. We need to give attention to managing our time well. Use some method to gain control of how time is spent.

The following is an outline of suggestions for time management:

Schedule Evaluation

1. Daily Time Record
- Keep a daily time record for seven (7) days.
- Choose a seven-day period when your activities will be normal for you.
- Duplicate the Daily Time Record. Keep seven copies on a clipboard or in a folder, one for each day of the week.
- Keep the clipboard or folder nearby.
- Record your activities in the five-minute squares as soon as you have an opportunity to do so.
- Use abbreviations you understand: (tel. = telephone; corr. = correspondence; cnsl. = counsel; tr. = travel; rd. ma. = read mail).
- Activities of extended time duration may be indicated by a word and a straight line extended through the correct time segments.
- Complete the Daily Time Record sheets for seven (7) days.

2. Daily Time Analysis
a. Identify various activities (Use a summary sheet.): (eating, telephone calls, writing, witnessing, studying, counseling).
b. Tabulate number of hours spent in each activity.

3. Daily Time Evaluation
a. Prioritize
Determine according to your priorities:
- Which activities involve too much time.
- Which activities involve too little time.
- Which activities need to be deleted.
- Which activities need to be delegated.
- Which activities need to be added.

b. Categorize—minimize time wasted in travel, switching from job to job, and so forth.
(1) Categorize various activities that should be grouped

together to be done on designated days or hours. Time can be saved by grouping things to be done within a certain geographical location. Make one trip instead of several. Some things need to be scheduled at given times because of the schedules of others.

(2) Categorize various activities that should be scheduled in sequences.

(3) Categorize various activities that should be scheduled at your times of highest productivity.

Schedule Planning

1. Long-Range Planning

a. Some things need to be scheduled several years in advance. Five- and six-year calendars are available.

b. Plan a yearly calendar.

Schedule major activities and priority events on your annual calendar at the beginning of the year.

c. Plan Monthly.

Briefly, at the end of each month, preview your schedule for the coming month.

2. Short-Term Planning

a. Weekly, fill in your schedule as completely as possible.

(1) Plan on Saturday or Sunday as accurately as you can.

(2) Schedule priority events, appointments, and activities.

(3) Give yourself time limits. Work expands to fill the time allotted to it.

(4) Schedule family time, free time, and so forth.

b. Daily, review your weekly schedule and plan your day.

(1) Make sure your priority activities are scheduled.

(2) Things to do.

(a) Write a "Things to Do" list.

(b) Number items on your list according to priority.

(c) Work items to be done into your schedule. (While you

are waiting, between major activities, use snatches of time.) Do things "on the way."

Concentrate on activities that need your full attention. However, with many activities you can do more than one thing at a time. (Example: As you travel, listen to tapes or use a minirecorder for dictation. Clear desk, go through junk mail, sign letters or papers while on the phone.)

(d) Tackle "Things to Do." Don't delay! Sometimes a five-minute job becomes a cloud of gloom over your head for days until it is done. Do the difficult ones first.

(e) Mark through items on your list as you get them done. Give yourself a pat on the back! That is satisfying.

(f) If you do not complete your "things to do" (and more than likely you will not), place the "leftovers" on your list tomorrow.

Schedule Management

1. Commit your time to God.

Matthew 6:33: "Seek ye first the kingdom of God."

Psalm 31:15: "My times are in thy hand."

Colossians 4:5: "Redeeming the time."

Whatever governs your time is your god. Time is the only thing we possess. What we do with it reveals what is first in our life.

2. Manage your schedule.

a. Do not allow your schedule to become your god.

b. Do discipline yourself for maximum effectiveness and fruitfulness.

3. Maintain an attitude of flexibility.

a. Interruptions will come.

Often these are divine interventions of opportunity.

b. Pray for discernment in accepting interruptions. They do not always need to be accepted.[4]

DIAGRAM 4.2
DAILY TIME RECORD

Date _____   Day _____

Morning					Afternoon						Evening				
7:00	**8:00**	**9:00**	**10:00**	**11:00**	**12:00**	**1:00**	**2:00**	**3:00**	**4:00**	**5:00**	**6:00**	**7:00**	**8:00**	**9:00**	**10:00**
:05	:05	:05	:05	:05	:05	:05	:05	:05	:05	:05	:05	:05	:05	:05	:05
:10	:10	:10	:10	:10	:10	:10	:10	:10	:10	:10	:10	:10	:10	:10	:10
:15	:15	:15	:15	:15	:15	:15	:15	:15	:15	:15	:15	:15	:15	:15	:15
:20	:20	:20	:20	:20	:20	:20	:20	:20	:20	:20	:20	:20	:20	:20	:20
:25	:25	:25	:25	:25	:25	:25	:25	:25	:25	:25	:25	:25	:25	:25	:25
:30	:30	:30	:30	:30	:30	:30	:30	:30	:30	:30	:30	:30	:30	:30	:30
:35	:35	:35	:35	:35	:35	:35	:35	:35	:35	:35	:35	:35	:35	:35	:35
:40	:40	:40	:40	:40	:40	:40	:40	:40	:40	:40	:40	:40	:40	:40	:40
:45	:45	:45	:45	:45	:45	:45	:45	:45	:45	:45	:45	:45	:45	:45	:45
:50	:50	:50	:50	:50	:50	:50	:50	:50	:50	:50	:50	:50	:50	:50	:50
:55	:55	:55	:55	:55	:55	:55	:55	:55	:55	:55	:55	:55	:55	:55	:55

Planning and Goal Setting

Meaningful time management will allow us to plan well and attain the goals of our lives. People are goal-oriented creatures. God has so constructed us. Without goals, a life will drift aimlessly.

Jesus was goal oriented. His whole life was a mission toward one goal. Over and again, the Scripture indicates that Jesus set His face toward Jerusalem. His goal was the cross and resurrection. Nothing would deter Him.

Paul was goal centered. He determined to go to Jerusalem. He purposed to go to Rome. The overall goal of his life is Philippians 3:7-14. Verse 14 concludes the passage: "I press toward the mark for the prize of the high calling of God in Christ Jesus." Paul pressed toward his goal.

Discouragement and depression take over an individual life when it has no goal. A church without goals simply drifts along, maintaining a status quo.

Many churches have no idea why they are there. We need to get a vision from God, then establish goals to fulfill that vision. The following are brief suggestions upon which the reader can enlarge:

1. Establish a vision. Leadership should challenge and guide the church in seeking God's vision for that church. Believe you can. Leadership should guide the church into the confidence that the church can do whatever God has a vision for the church to do.

2. Define priorities. Priorities may be stated in different forms. The broad outline of this book sets forth the threefold priority of a local church as follows: being the body of Christ, the church will . . .

Exalt the Savior;

Equip the saints;

Evangelize the sinner.

3. Set specific goals. Leadership should guide and involve

the church in setting specific goals to carry out the church's vision. These goals should fulfill the priorities.

Goals should be:
   Identifiable,
   Obtainable,
   Measurable,
   Challenging
   Involving all people.
   Develop two kinds of goals:

Long-range goals. An individual and a church will want to develop goals that extend for periods of five years and more.

Intermediate goals should be established. They should be challenging yet obtainable. Someone has said, "Nothing succeeds like little successes."

4. Plan definite steps.

Establishing goals accomplishes nothing unless steps to reach the goals are planned. Programs should be developed to reach these goals. Each program should be carefully planned to implement that particular program.[5]

In the next chapter, a Planning Sheet form has been provided to give guidance in developing a program. It is an excellent guide that will help you make sure every necessary step is taken in implementing a program.

Enlisting and Involving People

One of the great challenges in church life is that of enlisting and involving the members in the work of the Lord. The following are steps that may be used:

Pray

"Pray ye therefore the Lord of the harvest, that he will send forth laborers" (Matt. 9:38). Ask God to impress upon the hearts of those who need to be involved in this particular ministry.

Publicize

Make the need known. People do not respond to needs of which they are not aware. Make them aware of the needs.

Survey Membership Roll

Consider every member as a possibility. Ask the following questions:
- Where is this person now involved?
- Is this person morally fit?
- Is there a good reason that this person could not be involved?

Ask Individuals

General announcements and appeals get minimal response. Ask the individual to accept responsibility.

Present Challenge and Explain Requirements

- to small groups.
- to individuals.

Do not minimize the requirements. Be specific and detailed in explaining what the particular responsibility demands. Do not make it appear too difficult, but make it challenging.

Secure Commitment

Definite commitments must be secured for specific responsibility. For some involvements commitment may be secured that will terminate at a particular time. In some cases a person may be enlisted for a three-month period. She may have the understanding that at the end of that time she will have an opportunity to evaluate and continue or discontinue. This allows the individual to begin to serve on a "trial basis."

Train

- Set up training courses.
- Make individual study assignments.
- Use on-the-job training.

In some cases, specific training needs to be given before the person begins in his particular responsibility. In others, training may be given as he serves. Many people will never get the motivation to train until they start serving.

Stay Positive

If a person does not accept one place of responsibility, assure her that you are for her. Simply indicate to her that you will pray with her as she finds the place where God does want her to be involved.

Build Enthusiasm

Dr. Norman Vincent Peale has written an outstanding book entitled *Enthusiasm Makes the Difference*—and it does in the work of our Lord! The word *enthuse* comes from two Greek words: *en theos.* It means "in God." Enthusiasm is being in God and God in you. Enthusiasm is a faith attitude of trusting that God is in me and I am in God. God is working.[6] A great motto verse is Colossians 3:23: "Whatsoever ye do, do it heartily, as to the Lord, and not unto men."

Whatever you do, if it is really worth doing, put your whole heart into it. You can do that only as you do it "to the Lord." If you are doing it as unto people, there will be times when they do not approve. There will be times when people do not appreciate or congratulate. There will be times when rewards do not seem to come. If you are doing it as unto the Lord, you will continue on regardless of human response, regardless of rewards, regardless of human assistance, regardless of the cost.

Knute Rockne, the great coach of Notre Dame, is quoted as having said, "Give me a team with *P-E-P* and I'll give you a winner: P is for preparation, E for enthusiasm, P for persistence."

There are three basic ingredients for building enthusiasm. They are involvement, repetition, and reporting and sharing.

First, involvement.—People are enthused about the things in which they are personally involved. If you want to see people excited about your particular project, get them involved in some way. The goal of every pastor and church leader should be to involve the total membership in the life of the church. There should be something for every person to do.

At our Church Council meeting I challenged our leaders to work toward the time when we would no longer look for a person to fulfill a job, but seek a job for every person in our church. Every member should be involved in doing something in the Lord's work.

Second, repetition.—Many leaders think that they are compelled to say something different every time they speak. Some things must be said over and over again. To maintain enthusiasm about our priorities, we must be reminded of them constantly.

The pastor of a leading mission-giving church was asked, "How often do you preach on tithing?" He replied, "Every Sunday." Of course he did not preach a specific sermon on tithing every Sunday, but he included the principles of tithing and giving in every message. Repetition builds enthusiasm.

Third, reporting and sharing.—Excitement builds as people understand what is going on. When the people of a church are kept in the dark, enthusiasm wanes.

The Book of Acts is a reporting and sharing book. The Christians dispersed to do the work of witness of our Lord Jesus. Then they came together reporting and sharing what God had done. They shared the victories and struggles they experienced. This is how we got the Book of Acts. Dr. Luke wrote down the reports that had been shared.

In the churches I have pastored, our laypeople have been very enthusiastic about business meetings. It is a time of reporting and sharing what the Lord has been doing. Various leaders share projections, plans, and progress reports.

Business meetings ought to be a Spirit-filled exciting time in the life of a church. This is the time when we are following the vision that God has given us. We are making decisions about what to do and how to do it. Reports are given on the struggles and the successes.

People who lead at business meetings need to give exciting reports. Even though persons may have a mild and quiet personality, their reports build great enthusiasm.

Organization alone will not cause a church to grow. But growth will be severely limited without effective organization.

As Jesus is lifted up as Head of the church through effective biblical principles of organization and administration, a church will experience growth.

Questions

1. What internal problems must be addressed before your church can more effectively plan and set evangelistic goals?

2. What can be done to manage time more effectively?

3. What could you, as an individual, do to enlist and involve more people in the evangelistic growth of your church?

5 Exalt the Savior:

Through Program / Event Planning

The ministry of a growing church involves careful planning. Programs are developed in the light of priorities. They should be evaluated to make sure they fulfill the church's priorities.

A church has only so much time, energy, and resources. If a church is to grow, it cannot expend its resources on busywork. It cannot afford programs for their own sake.

Developing and Implementing a Program/Event

For meaningful program/event planning to take place, a definite procedure must be adopted to make sure every detail is covered. A written step-by-step procedure should be developed for every program/event of the church.

Business management uses various approaches to planning. Many of these approaches include some form of a flow chart which gives the chronological steps to be followed in a given program. Efforts are made to cover every detail of the plan.

In the pages that follow, we have taken business management procedures and adapted them to a local church's need. Utilizing planning sheets has been extremely meaningful for our own church and ministry.

Much time and frustration is avoided when planning sheets are used. Every step is written down. The program/

event is thought through with great care. Every step is covered. Nothing is left to chance. Each detail is assigned to a specific person. Deadlines are built into the planning.

Evaluation checkpoints are established throughout the program/event. Unless this kind of procedure is used, numerous steps may be overlooked in developing a program. The person responsible will have an uneasy feeling that something has been forgotten. And sure enough, when it comes to the time of the program/event, something has been forgotten.[1]

Program planning sheets should be filled out on everything the church does. They should be filed for future reference. Much time and effort can be saved by looking back to see each step that was taken in a given program. As the same or similar programs are planned in the future, what a fine resource this will be.

A secretary should have a planning sheet filled out on each of her responsibilities. For example, ordering church literature is a complicated procedure. When we filled out a planning sheet on ordering literature, we found that it required thirty-two steps. However, with the planning sheet, if the person who usually orders the literature is absent, someone else can move step by step through the procedure to order the literature.

There are many regular duties in the life of the church that need to be covered by a planning sheet. Some of them are wedding procedures, literature ordering, enrolling new Sunday School members, enrolling members of other organizations, baptismal procedures, Lord's Supper procedures, church newspaper mail-out procedures, and many others.

Developing and Utilizing a Planning Sheet

On the following pages are examples of planning sheets and how to use them (see diagrams 5.1-5.3). A planning sheet should cover a program or procedure from start to finish with such thoroughness that no detail is overlooked. The

SAMPLE PLANNING SHEET
OBJECTIVE/PLAN OR PROCEDURE: LOCAL CHURCH CRUSADE
(Jim Wilson — Larry McFadden)

P.S. NO.	STEP NO.	WHAT	WHO	WHEN	WHERE
100	19	Conduct Home Prayer Meetings	Stout, Gene Ortis	Oct. 4; 7:30 pm	Home
10	2	Promote Prayer in Depts. Organization and Comm. Mtgs.	Geo. Stout, Ev. Comm.	Aug. 6 & Following	Every Opportunity
130	25	Conduct 24 hr. prayer vigil	Ortis, Ev. Comm., Stout	Oct. 7	Church Audit.
125	24	Leadership Banquet	Ev. Com., B. Barnes	Oct. 7	Fellowship Hall
7	1	Develop Prayer List & Prayer Partners	Pastor	Aug. 2, 6	Church Service
35	6	Pers. Testimonies—Prayer for Revival S.S.	Stout, Ev. Comm. Gene Ortis	Sept. 10	
45	7	Preach on "How to Pray for Revival"	Pastor	Sept. 10	Worship Serv.
145	27	Reports to Paper	Barnes & Doug	During Meeting	
140	26	Hand out flyers—church groups	Ev. Com., Staff	During Meeting	Neighborhoods
20	4	Membership Letter (Mail out)	Jean, BeeGee, Volunteers	Sept. 5	From Church Office
60	9	Distribute Prayer Reminders	Mary Kent, Pat Parker, G. Ortis	Sept. 17	SS and Church Services
12	3	Arrangements—Motel, Auto, Meals		Sept. 1	Rodeway Inn
21	5	Secure Permission—School Assemblies	Dan Sampson	Sept. 6	
70	10	Operation "Andrew" Sunday	Ev. Comm., Pastor	Sept. 17	Worship Service
50	8	Mail out "Op. Andrew" Letter	Butch Thompson Phill Montgomery, L. Caster	Sept. 12	Church Office
93	17	Mail out to Leadership Banquet	Pastor, Jean S.	Sept. 29	Conf. Room
77	11	Mail Letter to Counselors	Bill Seavy, R. Hill	Sept. 19	Church Office
85	14	Mail out to Pew Packers	Linda Caster	Sept. 25	Conf. Room
80	13	Put out Banners-Signs (Church property & city)	M. Kent, Pat Parker, B. Barnes	Sept. 23	
79	12	Put Posters—Store Fronts	M. Kent, Bob B., Pat Parker	Sept. 23	Stores in Main Shopping Areas
87	15	Mail out Prospects	Mrs. Grace	Sept. 25	Conf. Room
90	16	Secure Newspaper Ads.	B. Barnes	Sept. 27	
120	23	Operation Doorstep	Brieden, Slay & Gaskins	Oct. 7	Neighborhoods
115	21	Phone city residents/invitation	Kent, Ev. Com. B. Barnes, P. Parker	Oct. 5-7	
117	22	Pass out flyers	Slay & Gaskins	Oct. 7	Shopping Center
110	20	Pass out flyers/H.S. & Int. Schools	Slay & Gaskins	Oct. 4-6	Schools
95	18	Pass out "JOY" Stickers	Kent, Parker, Youth Dir. G. Ortis	Oct. 1	Church Service
150	28	Follow-up	Doug McPherson Elson	During Meeting	In Homes

Using the following samples, develop your own planning sheet.

Summary Statements

As you will observe from studying the planning sheets, the examples are general. At various points in the planning sheet, the persons who have received specific assignments may need to develop planning sheets to cover their individual assignment. For example, in the planning sheet on the Crusade for Christ, separate planning sheets were filled out for such activities as Operation Doorstep, Leadership Banquet, and Home Prayer Meetings.

In planning the Crusade for Christ, periodic checkpoint meetings were held. Each week, the people who had received assignments came together for about thirty minutes for prayer and coordination. Communication and coordination are absolutely necessary if a program is to be effective.

A program planning sheet can be worked out by an individual or small group in a matter of thirty minutes to one hour. This is a wise investment of time. It will save much time and many headaches later. It will allow everyone to know what is going on. It will help you avoid the confusion of coming to a deadline and wondering what is going on because there has been no organization.

Presenting the Program/Event

Many otherwise effective programs die before they have ever begun because of a lack of effective presentation. Preparation with thoroughness is necessary for any planned program to be effective. But the presentation of the program with clarity and confidence is necessary if it is to be accepted by those to whom it is presented.

When I was a student at Baylor University, we lived in married-student housing. One afternoon there was a knock on our door. When I opened the door, I found myself facing

SAMPLE PLANNING SHEET

OBJECTIVE/PLAN OR PROCEDURE: LOCAL CHURCH CRUSADE
(Jim Wilson — Larry McFadden)

P.S. NO.	STEP NO.	WHAT	WHO	WHEN	WHERE
	1.	Develop Prayer List & Prayer Partners	Pastor	Aug. 2, 6	Church Service
	2.	Promote Prayer in Depts. Organization and Comm. Mtgs.	Geo. Stout, Ev. Comm.	Aug. 6 & Following	Every Opportunity
	3.	Arrangements—Motel, Auto, Meals	Bob Barnes	Sept. 1	Rodeway Inn
	4.	Membership Letter (Mail out)	Jean & BeeGee	Sept. 5	From Church
	5.	Secure Permission/School Assemblies	Dan Sampson	Sept.6	
	6.	Pers. Testimonies/Prayer for Revival/SS	Geo. Stout/Ev. Comm., G. Ortis	Sept. 10	
	7.	Preach on "How to Pray for Revival"	Pastor	Sept. 10	Worship Serv.
	8.	Mail our "O. Andrew" Letter	Butch Thompson, P. Montgomery, L. Caster	Sept. 12	Church Office
	9.	Distribute Prayer Reminders	Mary Kent, Pat Parker, G. Ortis	Sept. 17	SS & Church Services
	10.	"Operation Andrew" Sunday	Ev. Comm. Pastor	Sept. 17	Worship Serv.
	11.	Mail Letter To Counselors	Bill Seavy, Roland Hill	Sept. 19	Church Office
	12.	Put Posters—Store Fronts	M. Kent, Bob B. Pat Parker	Sept. 23	
	13.	Put out Banners—Signs (Church property & city)	M. Kent, P. Parker B. Barnes	Sept. 23	
	14.	Mail out to Pew Packers	Linda Caster	Sept. 25	Conf. Room
	15.	Mail out—Prospects	Mrs. Grace	Sept. 25	Conf. Room
	16.	Secure Newspaper Ads.	Bob Barnes	Sept. 27	
	17.	Mail out to Leadership for Banquet	Jean Smith	Sept. 29	Conf. Room
	18.	Pass out "Joy" Stickers	Kent, Parker, Yo. Dir., G. Ortis	Oct. 1	Church Service
	19.	Conduct Home Prayer Meetings	Stout, G. Ortis	Oct. 4-7:30 pm	Homes
	20.	Pass out flyers—H.S. & Int. Schools	L. Slay, E. Gaskins	Oct. 4-6	Schools
	21.	Phone city residents/Invitation	Kent, Ev. Com. B. Barnes, P. Parker	Oct. 5-7	
	22.	Pass out flyers	Slay & Gaskins	Oct. 7	Shopping Centers
	23.	Operation Doorstep	Brieden, Slay & Gaskins	Oct. 7	Neighborhood
	24.	Leadership Banquet	Ev. Com., B. Barnes	Oct. 7	Fellowship Hall
	25.	Conduct 24 hr. prayer vigil	Ortos, Ev. Comm. Stout	Oct. 7	Auditorium
	26.	Hand out flyers—church groups	Ev. Com., Staff	During Meeting	Neighborhoods
	27.	Reports to Paper	Barnes	During Meeting	
	28.	Follow-up	Doug. McPherson, Elson	During Meeting	In Homes

PRACTICE PLANNING SHEET

OBJECTIVE/PLAN OR PROCEDURE:
PERSON RESPONSIBLE:

P.S. NO.	STEP NO.	WHAT	WHO	WHEN	WHERE

PRACTICE PLANNING SHEET

OBJECTIVE/PLAN OR PROCEDURE:
PERSON RESPONSIBLE:

P.S. NO.	STEP NO.	WHAT	WHO	WHEN	WHERE

an almost comical situation. A young man was selling insurance door to door. He was evidently from one of the farms outside of town. Times were difficult. He had gotten a job selling insurance to try to make ends meet.

His very appearance suggested anxiety. He wore a black suit, probably the only suit he had. The pants were too short. The coat was too tight. His shirt and tie were outdated. His tie was pulled to one side under his collar.

He greeted me with a question. "You don't want to buy no insurance do you?"

My response evidently met his expectation. I replied, "I surely do not."

Many presentations like this young man's are offered in such a way as to elicit rejection. We need to plan our presentations and make them in a positive way that instills confidence.

On the following pages is a form for use in preparation of a program presentation and an example of such a presentation.

Outline for Presenting a Program/Event

Preparation

Preparation with thoroughness is necessary for effectiveness in any planned activity.

OUTLINE FOR PRESENTING A PROGRAM/EVENT

PROGRAM:

PURPOSE

PRESENT SITUATION:

PROPOSAL:

1. _____
2. _____
3. _____
4. _____

POSSIBILITIES:

1. Advantages:
   (1) _____
   (2) _____
   (3) _____
   (4) _____
2. Disadvantages:
   (1) _____
   (2) _____
   (3) _____
   (4) _____

PROJECTION:

Presentation

Presentation with clarity and confidence is necessary if it is to be accepted.

Plan

The Six-P Plan of Program Presentation

a. Program—Give name or title of the program. "I would like to share with you a proposal regarding _____ program."

b. Purpose—State the basic purpose or objective of the program concisely and clearly. "The purpose of this program is to _____ ."

c. Present situation—Describe the situation that now exists.

d. Proposal—Give in step-by-step order what is being proposed. Make sure you cover important details. The fewer questions that are left in the minds of the hearers, the more effective and acceptable your presentation will be.

e. Possibilities—Every program has two types of possibilities: positive and negative; advantages and disadvantages.

(1) List the advantages first. Through study, make sure the things you list are truly advantages. Include every advantage of your particular proposal.

(2) List the disadvantages. Disadvantages should be

thought through. There should be a compensating advantage to offset each disadvantage. If the disadvantages outweigh the advantages, the program may not need to be attempted. After stating each disadvantage, insert the word *however* and show how it is outweighed by the positive results expected, or show the answer you have offsets the disadvantage.

Example: "Disadvantage—This program will demand the expenditure of $XXX. However, the amount has been covered by a budgeted item. The size of the expenditure is justified because of the positive results expected in the following areas: _____

_____ ."

Why should the disadvantages be presented? Because of the following realities:

(a) If you do not present the disadvantages, your hearers will conclude that you have not thought through the program thoroughly.

(b) They may conclude that you are trying to deceive them. They may question your integrity.

(c) They may feel that you are trying to "put something over on them."

(d) By listing the disadvantages, you show that the program has been thoroughly thought through, that you are open and honest with the people, and that you have adequate answers for the disadvantages.

(e) Usually among your hearers there will be one or some who think from the negative perspective. They have made a habit of shooting holes in whatever is presented. By presenting the disadvantages, you cover that type of question before it is asked.

f. Projection—Set forth the first step that will need to be taken in carrying out the program. Indicate when it should begin.[3]

Ways for Presenting a Program/Event

1. It may be used simply to think through and study a given possible program for your own benefit.

2. It may be used to present a program to another individual or group.

3. It may be used in a family context to plan activities or involvements.

4. It may be used by supervisors. A supervisor may request a subordinate to submit a program presentation sheet on a particular proposal he is making.

Example: At one time the youth director of the church I was pastoring made a proposal of a change in the church calendar of activities. I asked him to work up a program presentation sheet. He was to present it to me when he had finished. He never mentioned the subject again. When I asked him about it, he indicated that after working up the program sheet he had come to realize that the proposal would not work. It had aided him to come to a good conclusion without his supervisor having to reject his proposal. For him, it was a morale builder. It helped him to learn to think for himself.

Ways to Use Outline for Presenting a Program/Event

Program: Deacon Ministry.

Purpose: To change the basic deacon ministry from Deacon Flock to Deacon Ministry Task Force Groups.

Present Situation: The church and deacons have, to a good degree, effectively used the Deacon Flock Ministry up to this point of membership growth (approximately 4,500 members). Beyond this point, a change in deacon ministry seems to be necessary if the church is to continue significant aggressive growth.

Concentration on special needs of ministry within the church seems to be a real need. To accomplish the special needs through our deaconship would be difficult with their present flock load.

At present we are experiencing a shortage of deacons to supply flocks as the church grows. It is becoming increasingly difficult to secure enough deacons to keep the flock number at twenty-five to thirty families. A larger number of families becomes overwhelming and unmanageable.

Proposal

1. That we drop the deacon flock assignments.
2. That we continue to have yokefellows assigned to each deacon for two purposes:
   a. To train and equip the yokefellow.
   b. To assist the deacon.
3. That Ministry Task Force Groups be organized within the deacon body. Each active deacon would serve on a task force group.
4. That all resident members be enrolled in a Sunday School class for small group fellowship and attention.
5. That the deacons annually serve as hosts for church-wide banquets. That the membership be divided equally among the deacons at that time for them to contact for the banquet.

Possibilities

1. *Advantages*

Deacons will be freed for service in more pressing areas of need. Some of these areas of need to which a Task Force Group could minister are:

   a. More effective follow-up with new members can be done by a deacon new-member group.

   b. Key prospects who have visited the church can be effectively ministered to by deacons.

   c. Other major needs for ministry can receive more

careful attention of the deacons. Such needs as prayer ministry, nursing-home visitation, crisis ministries, church absentees could well have deacon attention.

d. By being relieved of the flock responsibility, deacons can be free to participate more strongly in outreach and discipleship ministries of the church.

e. Deacons can be more available to equip younger members and new Christians if they do not have the flock responsibility.

f. Duplicate ministry is being done now by Deacon Flock and Sunday School teachers and workers.

2. *Disadvantages*

a. To drop the Deacon Flock Ministry would mean that the entire membership would not be assigned to someone for periodic contact, hence the increased chance of losing touch with some of our members. However, this is happening anyway as the flocks become larger. This need could be met by enrolling every resident member in a Sunday School class. The Sunday School would maintain contact with each member.

b. Annual deacon flock banquet has become a fellowship highlight of our church year; however, this can continue on a onetime annual contact basis by our deacons.

Projection: Establish deacon committee to work out organization for Task Force Ministries.

(You may use this outline to prepare your own program presentation sheets.)

Organizational Formula for Building a Church: Flake's Five Laws

During my seminary experiences I came to a new and exciting realization about how to build a great church through utilizing meaningful organization. As I shared earlier, during the first six years of my ministry I felt that giving emphasis to the spiritual life of the church and soul-winning was the only necessity in growing a great church.

While I was in seminary, a group of people who were starting a new church asked me to be their pastor. We began with thirty-two people meeting in an old school gymnasium in the heat of the summer. God richly blessed. We had a great spirit filled with enthusiasm. We secured a small building and began to grow. The church reached seventy-five in attendance. We were enthused.

But regardless of how much enthusiasm we had and how much we visited, we could not grow beyond about seventy-five in attendance. At that point, I enrolled in a religious-education class taught by Dr. Joe Davis Heacock at Southwestern Seminary. Dr. Heacock began to share about churches that had used organizational principles in growing. He showed by giving examples how churches, large or small, from every part of the world had grown through putting into practice these principles.

I was not very smart. But I was smart enough to know that my way was not working. Here was a man who said that he knew a way that would work. He proved it by examples. I decided to lead our church to utilize the principles he was teaching me. Before long, the church began to grow again. We grew to 100, then 125, then 140. By the end of two years, the church was stable financially and numerically. It has grown to an attendance of between 125 to 150. That was many years ago. That same church today is still strong and dynamic. It is one of our finest mission-support churches.

The principles Dr. Heacock presented were not new. They were set forth in 1915 by a layman named Arthur Flake from Mississippi. They have been called Flake's Five Laws of Sunday School Growth.

While these laws have been utilized for Sunday School growth, they apply to any organization within the church. In fact, if I were a businessman, I would use these same principles in building a business. They are basic organizational principles. The following is a list of the five laws of growth.

Discover the Prospects

Reaching people begins with locating specific individuals. We are not much concerned about people we do not know. As we discover prospects, we realize the possibilities. We begin to relate to them and to reach them.

Locating prospects is done in many ways—surveys, newcomers list, visitors in church, social functions, at weddings, funerals, from members, and so forth.

Provide the Space

a. A Sunday School (or any other church organization) will take the shape of the building in which it is housed.

Example: If no preschool department room is provided, few small children will be reached. If a ten-by-ten-foot room is provided for children birth through three years old, only five or six little ones will come. Young married couples will not be attracted to that church.

b. A church never grows to need space it fails to provide. Space must be provided before it can be filled.

c. A church will never consistently tax the capacity of the building space it uses. Surveys show that church attendance will level off at about 80 percent of maximum capacity. Occasionally the building may be packed. But the attendance will fall back, rise a bit, then fall back again. Before additional people can be reached, additional space must be provided. A church never uniformly fills the space allotted for Sunday School departments and classes. Some rooms may be filled to capacity while others are only half full. For the Sunday School to grow, additional space must be provided in spite of the fact that some rooms are not filled.

d. Space may be provided by remodeling, utilizing unused space, reassigning space for better utilization, acquiring adjacent buildings, multiple use of space, using offices, auditoriums or recreational facilities. In some cases, dual

Sunday Schools are used. Of course, another alternative is to build additional space.

e. A church should periodically study its space usage and make readjustments.

Enlist and Train the Workers

a. Surveys show that a ratio of ten additions in enrollment for each additional trained worker has held true for many years. If new people are to be reached, additional trained workers must be involved.

b. A continuous leadership training program should be in progress in the church.

Enlarge the Organization

a. Create new departments and classes. Develop a growth mentality throughout the church membership. Inflexibility limits the growth of a Sunday School. Teachers and members should not feel that a particular classroom is their own personal private property. For one group to insist on using a particular classroom when it would be more beneficial for another group can defeat the growth of the Sunday School. Teachers should lead the class members to be ready to take the necessary steps for the entire Sunday School to grow. Teachers should be glad to divide their classes in order to create new classes. They should make their classes a training group to supply additional workers throughout the church. Teachers should never try to hold on to class members.

Example: Our Sunday School had begun to grow. A group of older ladies were meeting in a classroom as I walked down the hall. When I looked in, they invited me to visit with them for a few minutes.

The teacher said, "Pastor, we're having an exciting time. We are ready to divide this class. We have a new teacher and group who are ready to start a new class. We are ready to let God use us to reach new people."

I responded, "That is great! I am not surprised. You are that kind of class."

The teacher smiled, "But we have not always been this way. It has not been long since I fought tooth and toenail against dividing this class. But I am convinced that we need to reach other people. I am ready."

Both classes grew so that the attendance was twice the size it had been in the one class.

New units grow more rapidly than existing ones. A new unit will ordinarily reach its peak growth within twelve to eighteen months. Percentagewise, smaller units will grow more rapidly than larger ones.

b. Utilize age grading as a basis for creating new units. Age grading is systematic. It recognizes natural growth and interest principles.

Go After the People

None of the above laws will hold true if a Sunday School does not visit. Weekly prospect visitation should be conducted by the Sunday School. We will discuss prospect visitation in Chapter 10.[4]

Programs will vary according to the needs and complexity of a church. A church should never begin a program simply because another church is doing it. Programs for their own sake will defeat the church's efforts for growth.

A church should study its own needs, the needs of its community, its potential and possibilities, then develop programs to fulfill its own mission. These should be carefully and effectively planned and implemented.

Evangelism and Stewardship Go Together

Faithful stewardship is one of the essentials for successful living and church growth. It is a giant step toward spiritual maturity when we learn that God is the absolute owner of everything. You can trust Him to supply every need. Life abounds as we learn to be givers rather than getters. Giving opens life's channels so that God can pour out His great blessings.

There are four kinds of giving taught in Scripture.

Systematic Giving (Tithing)

This involves bringing 10 percent of all income to God's house for God's work. Tithing is a principle revealed by God before He gave the law (see Gen. 4:4; 14:20).

Tithing was commanded by God (see Lev. 27:30).

Not tithing is robbing God and brings a curse (see Mal. 3:8-11).

Jesus commanded tithing (see Matt. 23:23).

Jesus receives our tithes through His body, the church (see Heb. 7:8).

The tithe is to be brought to God's house week by week (see 1 Cor. 16:2).

Spontaneous Giving (2 Cor. 8:7)

Spontaneous giving means seeing a need and responding by giving out of what you have to meet that need. The Good Samaritan gave like this in Luke 10:30-37. It is good to give to special offerings, to help the needy, or to assist in special ministries as needs arise.

Sacrificial Giving

This is the kind that gives until the life-style has to be changed in order to continue giving, to do without things that seem to be needed in order to give. An example of this kind is the widow and her two mites. She gave all she had and trusted God to supply her need. Without sacrifice there is no Christ-like living (see Matt. 16:24-25; 2 Cor. 8:5).

Spiritual Giving

This is "faith" giving. It is committing to God what you do not have, trusting Him to supply it. Your life becomes a channel through which He supplies needs. (See 2 Cor. 8:7.)

This kind of giving involves the law of sowing and reaping (see Gal. 6:7-9; 2 Cor. 9:6). It involves "hilarious" giving (see 2 Cor. 9:7). It means giving out of God's resources. (see Luke 6:38). Life becomes a channel, not a reservoir. Faithful stewardship on the part of God's people is God's method of supplying the resources for the church to fulfill the mission of Christ.

In summary, stewardship and evangelism are both evidences of obedience. Be faithful to God through your life, your witness, and your wallet.

Questions

1. What would hinder your church from using Flake's Five Laws of Sunday School Growth?

2. How could your church discover more evangelistic prospects?

3. If you ever needed to enlarge your church organization, where would you begin?

4. What will it take for your church to be more involved in going after people?

6 Equip the Saints:

The Heresy—Distinction Between Clergy and Laity

The function of the local church as the body of Christ is to exalt the Savior, equip the saints, and evangelize the sinner. As a church body lifts up Jesus as Head, the vitality of His life flows through the body. Individual members are drawn together into unity in the body. Members are equipped to live the Christ-life and to minister to build up the body. This provides a base for the pyramid of church growth.

As in the vine-branch analogy (John 15:1-8), the same blessed truth is presented. Jesus is the Vine. The church is the branches. The life of the Vine flows through the branches. The life force of the Vine produces fruit through the branches. By the faith union of abiding in Christ, the dynamic of His being permeates the church. Thus, the church is equipped and energized so that fruit bearing is a natural result.

In Acts 8:4, the laity, equipped with the fullness of the Christ-life, "were scattered abroad" and "went everywhere preaching the word." The New Testament pattern reveals Christ accomplishing His mission and ministry through lay-people who respond to His commission: "Go ye therefore, and teach all nations, baptizing them in the name of the Father, and of the Son, and of the Holy Ghost" (Matt. 28:19-20).

For a local church to function as a body of Christ, it must give itself to the equipping of members for the work of the ministry.

And he gave some, apostles; and some, prophets, and some, evangelists; and some, pastors and teachers; For the perfecting of the saints, for the work of the ministry, for the edifying of the body of Christ (Eph. 4:11-12).

Christianity Is a "Lay" Religion

A layperson is one who is not a religious professional. Laypersons do not earn their living by involvement in religious work. They earn their living in a "secular" occupation. But they serve their Lord with faithfulness.

All Christians are called to serve their Lord full time. There are no part-time Christians. "I therefore, the prisoner of the Lord, beseech you that ye walk worthy of the vocation wherewith ye are called" (Eph. 4:1).

Whether clergy or laity, every Christian is called to the "vocation" of ministry for the Lord Jesus, regardless of how one may make a living.

Jesus was not a religious professional. He was a carpenter by trade. He, too, worked with His hands to earn His bread. But His mission in our world was to fulfill His Father's will.

Jesus began His church by calling and commissioning laypeople. The professional religious leaders did not follow Jesus. The majority of them rejected Him.

He came unto his own, and his own received him not. But as many as received him, to them gave he power to become the sons of God, even to them that believe on his name (John 1:11-12).

He called people from every walk of life to follow Him. They were men, women, and young people who earned their living as fishermen, tentmakers, doctors, government officials, businessmen, and farmers.

Even the leaders of the church were not professionals in religion. They were called and gifted for leadership by God. As they followed Him, Jesus equipped them for leadership.

Peter and others were fishermen. Matthew was a tax collector. Luke, who followed later, was a physician.

Our Lord never intended for His apostles, evangelists, and pastors to become professionals. The leaders in our Lord's original church were not paid to do their job. Many had their physical and financial needs met through the support of those to whom they ministered. But they were not hired to do a job. They were called to walk with Jesus and minister to people. They did not serve for pay. God supplied their needs. He often did so through the people to whom they ministered.[1]

This is scriptural. The apostle Paul wrote in 1 Corinthians 9:9, "For it is written in the law of Moses, Thou shalt not muzzle the mouth of the ox that treadeth out the corn. Doth God take care for oxen?" Verse 14 says, "Even so hath the Lord ordained that they which preach the gospel should live of the gospel."

Every Christian is a minister. Some are involved as missionaries, evangelists, pastors, and teachers to the extent that they do not have time to earn their bread through a "secular" job. Others earn their bread through a job and minister in a life-style way for our Lord.

Churches often follow one of two extremes. They either overemphasize the clergy and minimize the laity, or minimize the clergy and overemphasize the laity. Either renders the church powerless. Both a God-called ministry of equippers and a fully involved body of laypeople are essential for a church to be effective.

The God-called leaders give oversight and equip the laity. The committed laity provides the great work force for fulfilling the ministry of the church. As they work together, the church is built up and the mighty work of God is accomplished.

Development of the Distinction
Between Clergy and Laity

Vitality continued in the life of the church during the apostolic period on into the second and third centuries. The great gospel explosion that began at Pentecost penetrated the world. Multitudes of churches were established. The New Testament pattern of church life continued.

By the latter part of the third century, gradual trends had developed that elevated the position of the bishops beyond the New Testament servant/leader role. As the church joined hands with the state, specific bishops came into places of prominence. Constantine, the Roman emperor, embraced Christianity. He made Christianity the official religion of the Roman Empire.

By the fifth century A.D., the bishop of Rome had gained ascendancy. This gave rise to the emergence of the Roman Catholic hierarchy with its papal system.

Gradually, there developed a strong elevation of the clergy and distrust of the laity. The Bible was taken out of the hands of the laity. It was felt that only the clergy could adequately understand it. Only the clergy could do the spiritual work of the ministry.

Such a departure from the Scripture gave rise to a multitude of heresies. This resulted in the spiritual decline of the Middle Ages. These were the Dark Ages of human history.[2]

Rediscovery of the Ministry of the Laity

In spite of the spiritual darkness of the Middle Ages, small groups of true believers followed the New Testament pattern. Those who followed New Testament principles during the Middle Ages were suppressed and often persecuted. They were driven underground. At times it appeared that the light of New Testament Christianity had been extinguished.

Then, in some unexpected place, it would appear again.

Through the centuries, groups like the Petrobrusians and the Waldensians practiced New Testament principles. When they were discovered, the leaders were sometimes killed, and the group dispersed. They would be driven underground.

The Renaissance was a movement that began within the universities in the late Middle Ages. There was rediscovery of the classics. There came a "revival of learning."

A thirst for the Scriptures began to grip the minds of many who were not within the clergy. In the middle of the fifteenth century, Gutenberg developed moveable type. The first book printed was a Bible.

Through the study of the Scriptures, spiritual restlessness led to reformation within the Roman Catholic Church. The Protestant Reformation developed as people revolted from the Roman Catholic Church. This brought a climate of greater religious freedom. Everywhere, little clusters of believers began to spring up. They held to the absolute authority of the Scriptures. They preached salvation by grace through faith. They practiced the priesthood of every believer.

God-called pastors emerged from among the laity. They worked in the fields and shops to earn their living. The distinction between the clergy and the laity was removed in these churches.

New Testament Christianity began to spread. The vitality of the churches increased evangelism. The nineteenth and twentieth centuries were characterized by a great emphasis on world missions.[3]

Reversion to Distinction Between Clergy and Laity in the Twentieth Century

In the twentieth century, though we adamantly claim doctrinal soundness concerning the priesthood of the believer, many churches practice the old heresy of distinction. We see five factors contributing to this distinction.

The noninvolvement of church members in ministry and witness shows this tendency. The willingness of church members to simply come, sit, and give money to pay someone else to do the work of the ministry and the witnessing of the church is a reflection of a return to the distinction.

Second, preachers attempting to do all the church's work of witnessing, soul-winning, counseling, and other "spiritual" ministries indicates a distinction between the clergy and the laity. Rather than equipping the laity for the work of the ministry, many preachers work hard attempting to do all the work of the church. They often become overburdened and face "burnout."

Third, we see it in the unrealistic expectation of churches toward their pastors. Many churches expect to pay the preacher to produce church growth. The preacher and paid staff are expected to do the spiritual work of the church.

Fourth, we see it in the tendency to resort to "gimmick" approaches to gather numbers and dollars. Rather than members being equipped to minister in order to see the church built up, spectacular events and gimmicks are often used to get attendance, members, and giving.

Fifth, we see it through some of the concepts of how to operate a church. We see it in some of the procedures of starting new churches. A group of people come together and decide to start a new church. They decide to "pool" their money. They hire a minister and expect him to do their ministering for them.

The preacher is paid to win the souls, do the witnessing, visit the sick, and so forth. The people attend, listen to sermons, and give their money. If the church grows, they hire another minister to help the first minister to do the ministering. This is a reversal of New Testament church life.

Reasons for the Distinction

The responsibility for reverting to a distinction between clergy and laity can be laid at the feet of both pastor and people. The people have all too often been ready to yield their spiritual responsibility to the people. The pastor has been all too ready to assume the spiritual responsibility for the people.

People Reasons

There are three reasons for such behavior by the people. The first reason is ignorance of the Word of God and spiritual immaturity. People often do not understand that when they were saved, they became God's ministering people.

The second reason is the absorption of the people with the world. Many church members become totally occupied with making a living and involvement in the world. They have no time or energy left for their ministry. They say, "Let George (the hired minister) do it. That is what we pay him for."

The third reason is that many have religion rather than a relationship. Some church members never witness or serve because they do not truly know Jesus Christ. Theirs is a religion rather than a relationship with Christ.

Pastor Reasons

There are five reasons with reference to the pastor for a reversion to the distinction between clergy and laity.

The first reason is ignorance. Some pastors are ignorant of the New Testament ministry of the pastor and laity. They have not studied the Word to determine the biblical pattern of ministry for the church and pastor.

The second reason is pride. A pastor may come to enjoy a pedestal position. The place of an authoritarian ruler or the "super saint who can do it all" may appeal to his ego.

The third reason is pressure. There is a great amount of pressure on a pastor to meet the expectations of people. Some simply yield to the pressure of the people to fit into their mold. People who are ignorant of the equipping ministry expect the pastor to do it all.

The fourth reason is expediency. Equipping the laity is a

difficult task. It is time-consuming. It does not happen quickly. Sometimes it is easier to "do it oneself" than to discover, enlist, and equip someone else to do it.

The fifth reason is shortsightedness. A preacher may have ambition for immediate numerical results. With enthusiasm and energy, a preacher can win a certain number of people to Christ and bring them into the membership of the church alone. Equipping the laity seldom brings short-term success. Effectiveness is seen over a longer period of time. A pastor must personally witness, but if he does not equip the members of the body to do so few people, comparatively speaking, will be saved.

A reversion to the distinction between the clergy and laity brings ruin into God's church. It defeats His plan. Such a practice brings fivefold ruin.

A human plan is substituted for the divine plan. The blessing of Christ in its fullness does not rest on the ministry in such cases. Human wisdom falls far short of what God would do.

The ministry of the church is limited to the ministry of a few paid staff members rather than multiplied by as many members as belong to the church. The "great army" of the church sits idle while the generals go out into battle. Only a small percentage of the potential of the church is reached.

The pastor spreads himself too thin. He has too much to do. He has too little help. Soon he becomes exhausted and ineffective. The work of the church is defeated.

The church does not mature. Maturity comes as members of the church are involved in ministry. The involvement of members builds the church into the "measure of the stature of the fullness of Christ" (Eph. 4:13). Growth within the body does not take place. The church is defeated.

The multitudes go untouched and unreached. Only a small percentage of the people who could be reached by the entire church are actually reached. Our world will never be reached by religious professionals. It will be reached as the great masses of church members are equipped and involved in ministry and witness.

The hope of the church's fulfillment of the mission of Jesus in our world is for pastors and people to return to the New Testament pattern of ministry. Pastors and other God-called leaders must equip the saints for the work of the ministry to build up the body of Christ.

Questions

1. Discuss what you believe to be the primary role of the pastor related to evangelistic church growth; then discuss the primary role of the laity related to evangelistic church growth.

2. Which statement best describes your church and why?
    a. Overemphasize the clergy and minimize the laity
    b. Minimize the clergy and overemphasize the laity
    c. God-called leaders equip the laity

7 Equip the Saints:

Hope—Equipping Ministry

The effectiveness of the church is minimized when it reverts to the old heresy of distinction between the clergy and the laity. This is the least negative result. The usual result is a climate of spiritual deadness. A church becomes more of a social organization than a radiant, life-filled body of Christ.

Church growth comes from within. The biblical principle of equipping the people of God is the hope of the church. It is the church's hope for being built up within by the dynamic of the Christ-life. It is the church's hope for fulfillment of the mission of Jesus in our world.

Pattern for the Equipping Ministry

He led captivity captive, and gave gifts unto men. . . . He gave some, apostles; and some, prophets; and some, evangelists; and some, pastors and teachers; For the perfecting of the saints, for the work of the ministry, for the edifying of the body of Christ (Eph. 4:8,11-12).

Let us examine the word meanings and the structure of this passage.

"He"—This is Jesus who led captivity captive through His death on the cross and resurrection. Now that He has ascended, He has given through His Holy Spirit gifts unto people.

"Gifts"—These are special bestowals of grace to enable and equip individuals for leadership and ministry.

"Apostles"—Literally, "One who is sent out from the Lord." Many think that the modern equivalent would be the missionary who crosses cultural lines to introduce Christianity where Christ has never been known.

"Prophets"—Those who receive a message from God and declare it to persons. They are often used of God to confront God's people with their sins and to call them to repentance. The modern understanding of the word is to foretell. This element is included in the work of the prophet biblically. But, primarily his mission is to "forthtell."

"Evangelists"—Those who are instrumental in getting the good news of the gospel to the lost. The evangelist is directly involved in reaching the lost. The evangelist also encourages and equips members of the body to reach the lost.

"Pastors"—Those who shepherd, nurture, and feed the flock of God.

"Teachers"—Those who study, understand, systematize, and guide others to understand the truth of God.

"Pastor-teacher"—could be one and the same office.

"Perfecting"—equipping, fitting, getting ready.

"Saints"—the set-apart ones, God's people, Christians.

"Word"—labor, toil, business.

"Ministry"—(Greek—*diakonias*) service.

"Edifying"—to build up, as a carpenter builds a house.

"Body of Christ"—the church.

The equippers (apostles, prophets, evangelists, pastors, and teachers) are given to fit—equip—each and every one of God's people. The people of God (members of the body) are to do the work of ministry. The result of their doing that work is that the body of Christ will be built up.[1]

These five types of leadership gifts are given for equipping. They are for the purpose of outfitting Christians to do the tasks assigned to them. All five are given to the church. The pastor/teacher seems to be the one who remains with a particular local church. Apostles, prophets, and evangelists are gifts given to the body but often move from one local church to another to assist in ministry.

Equipping is the Greek word *katartismos*. From it comes the English term *artisan*, an artist or craftsman. The term is used in the New Testament for "mending" the nets. It is used when fishermen mend their nets to prepare for fishing.[2]

In the church, members are to be outfitted, prepared for the work of the ministry. Those who have equipping gifts are provided to the church in order to outfit all the Christians for their work of ministry.

All Christians are to be involved in the work of ministry. They are to be equipped for that work of ministry. Equipping and involvement need to be simultaneous. Equipping will not be productive unless some type of involvement is present simultaneously.

Seldom does a person have the motivation for being equipped unless she is involved already in some measure. Equipping cannot be isolated from involvement. As a person is more thoroughly and effectively equipped, she will become more involved.

The result of members of the body being equipped is that the church will be edified. *Edify* is a carpenter word. It means "to build up." The figure is that of a carpenter building a house. First, he lays the foundation. Then, he puts up the walls and the roof. He builds up the house until it is complete.

As members of the church are equipped for the work of ministry, the body of Christ is built up. The "building of God," the church, is built up as stone after stone is laid upon the foundation.

Through the ministry of the laity, the church is built up in two ways: first, in maturity, The church grows into the measure of the stature of the fullness of Christ. Second, the church is built in number. Through the ministry of the laity, the lost are brought to Christ. They are added to the church. The number is built up.

Biblical Pattern of Equipping

The following pages are examples of two types of church life. The first example represents the *world's way* of operating a church. The second represents the scriptural strategy.

The World's Way

The world's methods of equipping have invaded the church (see diagram 7.1). The world and many church members look at "church" as simply another activity tacked on to a busy life. We live in the world, engaging in numerous activities. We go to work, to the civic club, to school, to social activities, and to church. Church is simply one of many involvements. We may spend one hour or several hours each week going "to church." Church is another activity to attend.

Such a concept of church is totally unscriptural. Church is *people*! It is people who have received their life from Jesus Christ, who are sharing that life in fellowship with one another, and who are reaching out to extend that life to others.

The world's way of operating a church has the professional clergy doing the "spiritual" work. "Religious George," the hired minister, does the work of the ministry. The pastor has the ministry. The people do not have a ministry. They merely give to pay the bills.

The pastor ministers to the church members. He attempts to edify and build up the people of God. They simply give and pay him a salary. But they do not become involved in the work of the ministry.

The pastor reaches out to the lost in evangelism. On the one hand, he ministers to and edifies the church members.

On the other hand, he is busy reaching out to a lost community. The members do not witness. They are not involved in reaching people.

Of course, the pastor cannot do all the work of evangelism and see the church grow. Therefore, he invites other professionals to assist. He secures a staff. He invites a professional evangelist to come in and reach people for the church. The specialist is publicized. Appeals are made to get a crowd. The specialist preaches effectively and many people are brought into the church.

What does the membership do? They come! They give! They pay the bills! This is the world's way! It defeats New Testament Christianity! It is a reversal of the biblical pattern for church life.

The Scriptural Strategy

In the biblical pattern of church life, members live in a context of fellowship with one another (see diagram 7.2). The people are the church. They do not simply attend church. Whether gathered or scattered, members of the body live in the context of fellowship with one another. From that fellowship members move out into a world on mission for Christ. The member moves out into the business world on mission for her Master. Wherever she goes, she *is* the church—reaching, touching people for the Lord Jesus Christ. A member moves in and out of his business world, social world, school, and neighborhood on mission for Jesus.

In the biblical pattern of church life, the pastor is involved in the equipping ministry. The ministry belongs to the church. Every member is a minister. The pastor equips the members, so they become effective in ministry. Thus, together, pastor and people cooperate and complement one another in fulfilling the ministry of the church.

Diagram 7.1

The World's Way

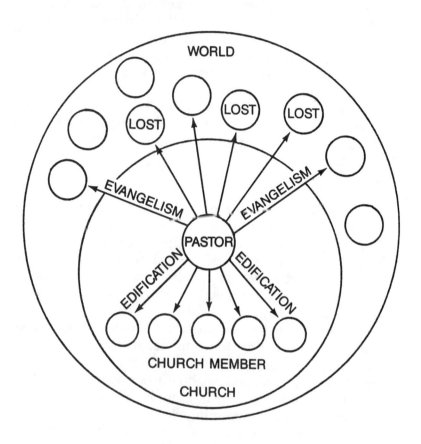

The congregation hires a minister to do its work of minisry and evangelism. The pastor is charged with the full-time task of shepherding and teaching the flock. The members are not involved in identifying one another. The pastor does the work of evangelism. The members are not involved in direct or personal evangelism.

Diagram 7.2

Scriptural Strategy

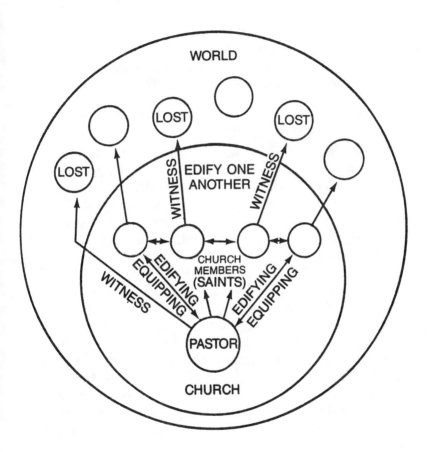

Pastor equips, teaches, trains, and inspires members of the church. Church members build up one another. Church members witness and lead the lost to Christ. Pastor, as a Christian, personally witnesses. He is an example to the church in witness.

Because members are equipped for the work of ministry, they touch the lives of lost people outside the church in a meaningful way. Through their witness the lost are brought to Christ. Every Christian is a witness. The entire membership is involved in the work of evangelism.

While the pastor equips the saints, he is also directly involved in witness for Christ. He reaches the lost through his pulpit ministry, and also through personal witness. The pastor cannot do all of the witnessing of the church, but he must witness.

Personal Witness of the Pastor

There are three reasons the pastor must witness. First, witness is a natural expression of his own life. No pastor can know the victory of spiritual power apart from consistent life-style witnessing for Jesus. If he does not share Christ personally with people, he will certainly not be effective when he comes to the pulpit on Sunday morning. Personal witnessing keeps the pastor in touch with people. It feeds his life with spiritual nurture and joy.

Second, lost people need to be saved. Some people can be reached only by the pastor. He must be available to let Jesus touch other people through him in a life-style way.

Third, the pastor is an example to the flock of God. Members seldom become significantly involved in witness apart from the leadership of the pastor. The pastor's witness is a model for the membership of the church. He not only instructs them in witness, but demonstrates witness to them through personal life-style. They observe his attitude, spirit, and techniques.

It is a happy church that is involved in the scriptural strategy of operation in church life. It becomes a healthy, growing church. Pastoral leadership and lay membership work together in fulfilling the mission of Christ for His body. The church is built up qualitatively as it matures into the "measure of the stature of the fullness of Christ" (Eph.

4:13). It is built up quantitatively as new believers are led to Christ and added to the church.

Role of the Laity

To prepare God's people for works of service, so that the body of Christ may be built up (Eph. 4:12, NIV).

The laity does the work of the ministry. God has gifted each member with all that is necessary for him to fulfill his ministry.

What a joy Christians discover when they begin to use the gifts God has given for the work of ministry! Life becomes meaningful and fulfilled. A layperson may have as strong a ministry as any preacher. She may make a living at a "secular" job. But, it is not "secular." It is spiritual, because everything a Christian does is spiritual. She may be working at a job for eight to ten hours a day for a certain employer, but on that job she is serving God. The Christian is on mission for Jesus Christ—a life-style witness. The believer uses personal spiritual gifts in the world to make a contribution to society and to minister to people at the point of their need. The Christian is on mission in the world to touch people for Jesus Christ.

In the context of the organization of the church, the Christian utilizes his particular gift in ministry. God has gifted all members so that every gift is present in the body that is necessary for the church to be complete. The church possesses every gift it needs to fulfill its mission for Jesus.

Arrangement of Members in the Body

Members are arranged in the body of Christ by God's design. "But now hath God set the members every one of them in the body, as it hath pleased him" (1 Cor. 12:18).

But speaking the truth in love, may grow up into him in all things, which is the head, even Christ: From whom the whole body fitly joined together and compacted by that which every joint supplieth, according to the effectual working in the measure of every part, maketh increase of the body unto the edifying of itself in love (Eph. 4:15-16).

God has joined the members of the body one to another in such a way that each complements all the others to make up a full, complete body of Christ. Each member has received gifts. These gifts put together form one organism—the body of Christ.

In the analogy of a human body, the interrelationship of gifted members is the emphasis. There is diversity of membership. None is like any other. Yet, diversity is essential to unity. If all members function, the church thrives. If any does not, the church suffers.

Spiritual Gifts

In the examination of spiritual gifts, various lists have been set forth. Some biblical interpreters have listed nineteen gifts, others twenty-seven gifts, still others present various other numbers and clusters of gifts.

Four New Testament passages list separate gifts. These passages are Ephesians 4:11; Romans 12:6-8; 1 Corinthians 12:28-30; and 1 Peter 4:8-10.

God gives these gifts to the body to supply every need and to fulfill every function. The following is a list of nineteen gifts and a brief interpretation of them:

(1) *Apostles*—Those sent out on a mission from our Lord. Some apply this to missionaries who cross cultural barriers with the gospel.

(2) *Prophecy*—Those who receive a message from God and declare it.

(3) *Evangelists*—Those who bear the good news of Jesus to the lost.

(4) *Pastors*—Those who feed and nurture the people of God.

(5) *Teaching*—The ability to clarify God's truth. To understand it and present it to others in such a way that they can understand.

(6) *Ministry*—Helps: an ability to serve, to meet needs, to help.

(7) *Exhortation*—An ability to encourage others, to stimulate them to action.

(8) *Government, Ruling, Leading*—An ability to administer programs, to organize, to lead people.

(9) *Mercy*—The ability to discern needs in the lives of others and to feel for and with others; sympathy.

(10) *Giving*—The ability to earn money and to give it to the right places at the right time in God's work.

(11) *Miracles*—The ability to be used of God in mighty, supernatural works and occurrences.

(12) *Healing*—The ability to be used of God to minister to the physical, emotional, and spiritual needs of a person.

(13) *Tongues*—The ability to speak another language, using it to communicate the gospel.

(14) *Interpretation of Tongues*—The ability to interpret languages.

(15) *Discerning of Spirits*—The perception to know the true attitudes and spirit of a person.

(16) *Words of Wisdom*—The ability to understand and apply what one knows; to do and say the right thing.

(17) *Words of Knowledge*—The ability to understand and know facts and details that are not apparent.

(18) *Faith*—The ability to believe God and to allow God to work mightily.

(19) *Hospitality*—The ability to receive people, to entertain and minister to their needs.[3]

There is no evidence that this list of gifts is meant to be conclusive. There may well be many other gifts God gives that body for His service. There are most certainly differing arrangements or clusters of gifts in individual members' lives. Regardless of the gift, the purpose is for the building up of the body of Christ.

Role of Pastor and Staff in Equipping Ministry

To equip "the saints" (Eph. 4:12).

"Commit thou to faithful men, who shall be able to teach others also" (2 Tim. 2:2).

One of the chief duties of the pastor is to assist every member in discovering and developing in the ministry God has for him. This is priority for the pastor and pastoral staff.

The procedures used in the equipping ministry are manifold. First, God-anointed pulpit preaching guides the direction of the church. Pulpit fire proclaiming the Word produces conviction, calls to repentance, and results in surrendered lives.

The challenge of pulpit exhortation stimulates and motivates members of the body to obey Christ. The direction of the equipping ministry is established and guided through the preaching ministry of the pastor.

Second, personal enlistment of individuals in particular ministries is a must. The pastor, staff, and lay leaders of the church must give attention to individual members in discovering their gifts and in enlisting them in ministries that will utilize the gifts. The nominating committee or group within a church responsible for enlisting workers should have as their purpose to enlist every member of the church for service. Instead of taking the approach of attempting to secure a person to fulfill each job, the approach of finding a job for every member should be used.

Howard was a new convert. He was a sergeant in the air force. He knew little about the Bible and theology. But he was a people person. He had a warm smile and a friendly handshake. Howard was enlisted as a greeter for the church services. Visitors would come, receive a friendly greeting, and be seated. At the end of the service, Howard would shake their hands again and call them by name. Visitors would return. They would remark about the friendly atmosphere of the church.

Howard later became a teacher, then a deacon. But first he became a greeter in the church. This was something he could do in beginning to minister. He consistently shared Christ in his marketplace.

Third, training in techniques and methods is essential for equipping people. Seminars, classes, on-the-job training, and other approaches must be used to train people for particular ministries.

Over a period of eight years, we conducted forty-seven witness-training schools of several sorts. Through this means, many laypeople were trained to witness for Jesus Christ. They were not only taught the Scriptures but trained in methods of presenting the claims of Christ.

Fourth, God has set forth as His basic method for equipping Christians that of teaching the Scriptures. God's method is given to us in 2 Timothy 3:16-17: "All scripture is given by inspiration of God, and is profitable for doctrine, for reproof, for correction, for instruction in righteousness: That the man of God may be perfect, thoroughly furnished unto all good works."

All Scripture is God breathed. It is filled with the very power of God. Scripture is profitable. It is useful. The usefulness of Scripture is not simply for winning a debate. We do not study Scripture simply to know the facts of it. Scripture is useful in knowing how to live. It tells people how to be saved. It tells saved people how to live the "abundant life" effectively. It thoroughly furnishes a person for good works. It equips a person to do the work of God.

Four verbs are used to show us how Scripture is useful. It *teaches* us what God requires. It *reproves*, convicts us of where we are wrong. It *corrects*—"stands us up straight." It *instructs* in the right way to live.

Teaching Scripture is the primary method for equipping God's people for the work of the ministry. Scripture is our complete set of resources for living an effective life. It is to be taught from the pulpit, in the classroom, and in personal instruction.

Different approaches are needed by different people for Scripture to become meaningful in their situations. In 1 Thessalonians 5:14-15, five aspects of biblical counsel are seen. They are given to us in the form of five verbs. In the context of a church body, all of these are present. Different situations will demand different approaches. When the church body is skilled in the utilization of the Scriptures for ministry, the different approaches are used to meet the need of an individual.

> Now we *exhort* you, brethren, *warn* them that are unruly, *comfort* the feebleminded, *support* the weak, *be patient* toward all men. See that none render evil for evil unto any man: but ever follow after that which is good, both among yourselves, and to all men (1 Thess. 5:14-15, author's italics).

Examine the five words:

Exhort (parakaleo)—means "to beseech, exhort, encourage, or comfort." The word is sometimes used to refer to the Holy Spirit. Literally it means "to call alongside of." References to it are found in Romans 12:1; 2 Corinthians 1:4; and Romans 15:30.

Warn (noutheteo)—meaning "to put in mind, to warn, to confront." It is intended to produce a change in life-style. References where this word is used are Romans 15:14; 1 Corinthians 4:14; and Colossians 3:16.

Comfort (paramutheomai)—meaning "to cheer up, to encourage, or to comfort." One encourages the fainthearted or discouraged. Reference is 1 Thessalonians 2:11.

Support (antechomai)—meaning "to cling to, to hold fast, to take an interest in, to hold up spiritually or emotionally." It expresses mutual trust and interdependence. References are Titus 1:9 and 1 Thessalonians 5:14.

Be patient (makrothumeo)—meaning "to be patient or to

have patience." References are in Matthew 18:26-29; James 5:7; and Hebrews 6:15.

The Scripture given through the counsel of a Christian and a church body meets the needs of individuals. Individuals approach others at the point of their need armed with the power-filled Word of God which is itself the sword of the Holy Spirit.[4]

Possibilities for Involvement

Many areas of ministry for our Lord exist for the layperson. Every member of the church should be involved in some area of ministry. Areas of ministry exist both inside and outside the church.

Every member should be involved in the outreach ministry of the church. The secular jobs through which laypeople earn their living are mission fields. Through a life-style of witness, laypeople do their greatest work. They have contact with people that preachers and church staff workers have no opportunity to touch. As laypeople share Christ with them at the point of their need, they are brought to a saving knowledge of the Lord Jesus. They are brought into the life and fellowship of the church.

Laypeople participate consistently in the organized program of evangelism. They serve in an organized effort to make sure that every person in the community receives the witness of the Lord Jesus Christ.

Laypeople serve in the discipleship and Bible-teaching ministry of the church. A ready-built approach to discipleship is through the Sunday School. Every teacher should be a leader in discipleship. The teacher should organize the class into groups for ministry and discipling.

There are unlimited opportunities for service ministry within the church. Through the body life of the church, God's people share with one another. Deacons assist the pastor in shepherding the flock and in ministering to the people. Yokefellows are people who are not ordained. They are enlisted to assist the deacons in ministry. In doing so, they supply valuable service. They grow through their experience of ministry.

Ministry Opportunities

As a church identifies the needs within the body and in its community, an unlimited number of ministry opportunities exist. Some of these are:

New member follow-up: Each new member needs to be assisted in Christian growth and in becoming a part of the life of the church.

Visitor follow-up: Each person who visits the church should have a follow-up visit by someone in the church.

Church membership attendance: Church absentees need to be visited to discover their need, to be ministered to, and to reclaim them.

Hospital visitation: Members and prospects in the hospitals should be visited by church members.

Homebound and nursing home ministry: People who are isolated from the body life of the church need to be visited and ministered to by the people of the church.

Personal caring ministry and witness in the marketplace: Every Christian is on mission for Christ in the marketplace and in all of life!

Crisis ministry: Individuals and families need the ministry of church members during crisis experiences in their lives.

Bus ministry: There is some area of service in the bus ministry in which any member can serve. These include visiting people on bus routes, assisting by riding the bus or by driving a bus. Assistance can be given in visiting and counseling bus ministry parents.

Committee service and task-force groups: Any church can establish various committees and task-force groups to meet needs in the organizational life of the church. Committees should not be set up simply to give people positions. They should be set up to meet needs. Also, they give members an opportunity to actively serve.

A church may have numerous committees. Some of these are: building, grounds, finance, fellowship, personnel, benevolence, ushers, greeters, nominating, baptism, Lord's Supper, music, education, evangelism, missions, and any number of others.

Leadership ministries can involve numbers of people as leaders in various organizations of the church such as missions, Sunday School department directors, music ministry, and so forth.

Teaching ministries involve laypeople in teaching Bible classes. Small-group Bible studies in the Sunday School involve a maximum number of teachers. Home Bible studies and extension Bible studies involve others.

Essential to the equipping ministry of the church is the total involvement of its membership in ministry.

Elevate Ministry and Witness

Total involvement of the membership in leadership ministries and in the organizational structure of the church is unrealistic. Not every member can be a deacon, teacher, or a committee member. But every Christian *can* be involved in ministry and witness. The church needs to elevate the role of every Christian as a participant in caring ministry and witness. Ministry and witness should be given equal recognition to a leadership role.

Ministry includes needs-based small groups that meet felt needs in the name of Christ. The church must be meeting needs to earn credibility for witness. The Bible instructs us to witness. Ministry can increase the effectual reception of our witness.

People Sharing Jesus in the Marketplace

The following are examples of Christians who make a living in various ways, but whose vocation is the work of the ministry of Jesus.

• A service-station operator pumps gasoline and services automobiles. At the same time, he shares Jesus with people.

• A school principal teaches a men's Bible class. He leads the class in building disciples. They have reached and discipled men with alcohol, social, family, and other problems.

• An elderly woman confined to a wheelchair goes down the list of names in the telephone directory to call people and share Jesus with them. She graciously uses a religious survey approach to determine their interests. Many are interested in Jesus. She shares as deeply as they desire to go. She gives their name to the church for follow-up.

• A dentist and his wife devote themselves to a newcomer ministry. They visit newcomers to the community, welcome, and assist them in getting acquainted. Of course, they witness and attempt to lead them to find a church home.

• A bank executive talks to people about their finances. He realizes that financial problems often have spiritual roots. He attempts to share Christ with each person who sits down at his desk. He is very active in his church and denomination. This particular man has probably influenced more lives for Christ than any preacher in his city.

• A school custodian serves on the benevolence committee. After his work hours each afternoon, he makes benevolence and other visits. He learned to use John 3 in witnessing. He leads many people to personal faith in Christ. He guides many people to follow Christ in church membership.

• A plant shift worker attends each service of the church while not on his job. On his five days off, he and his wife use their time for special witness, service, or mission projects.

• A retired university professor commits himself to lay evangelism-equipping ministries. He consistently wins souls through the outreach of his church. He teaches *WIN: A Lay Evangelism Strategy* Schools in many other churches. He is instrumental in equipping laypeople to share Christ.

● A Christian counselor uses his gifts to help people with needs. He uses his abilities and preparation for the ministry of the Lord in his church.

● A retired armed-services person uses his administrative gifts to direct and build a Sunday School department. He is effective in putting his gifts and training to work for the glory of Christ and the good of the church.

● An electrical engineer uses his gifts helping with the church's maintenance needs. He saves his church thousands of dollars each year through his personal time contribution.

Incorporating New Members into the Life of the Church

One of the great resources of the church is its new members. Each new member needs to be incorporated into the life of the church. New members should be involved not only in fellowship but also in service. They need to be guided into the life of the church. They need to be nurtured and discipled.

Several steps can be taken to incorporate new members into the life of the church.

1. When the decision is made: Counsel with the new member should come immediately as the decision to unite with the church is made public.

2. Immediate personal follow-up. Within twenty-five hours the new member should be visited, counseled, and instructed. The church should have a New Member Packet that explains about the life of the church, how to live the Christian life, how to establish prayer time and family altar, and gives guidance into the various organizations or groups in the church.

3. Letter of welcome, encouragement, and instruction.

The pastor should write each new member a letter of welcome. He should invite them to attend the New Member Fellowship Class.

4. Deacon visit. A new member can be assigned to a deacon or some other member for personal nurture.

5. Sunday School visit. The appropriate Sunday School department should be notified. The Sunday School should enlist the new member as quickly as possible in a class.

6. New member reception and classes. Periodically, a church should have a new member reception. It should be a get-acquainted time. It should be a time when the life, ministry, and direction of the church is shared with the new member. The reception can be the first in the series of several new member classes. The new member should be contacted each week and encouraged to participate in that week's new member class.

I have used the following series of studies for new members entitled *How to Be a Growing Christian:* (1) The Church, The Body of Christ; (2) Salvation from Start to Finish; (3) Growing the Christian Life; (4) Living the Victorious Life; (5) Doctrine; (6) Can a Saved Person Ever Be Lost? (7) Missions, Our Mandate.

The Happiness of an Equipping Ministry

It is a happy church that recognizes the value of equipping its members for the work of the ministry. Blessed is the life and the church that follows the biblical pattern of equipping in the church life.

In such a church there is maximum joy. When every member fulfills the mission and instruction of the Head, the Lord Jesus, the body is filled with vitality and health. Joy characterizes the life of the individual member. It radiates through the life of the church.

Equipping the people of God brings maximum fruitfulness. Jesus promised that if His own abide in Him, they will bring forth much fruit. Abiding is obedient participation in the Christ-life. As a church body abides in Jesus, maximum fruit results.

> He shall be like a tree planted by the rivers of water, that bringeth forth his fruit in his season; his leaf also shall not wither; and whatsoever he doeth shall prosper (Ps. 1:3).

Equip the saints for the work of the ministry.

Questions

1. Discuss the contrast between "the world's way" and "scriptural strategy" for evangelistic church growth.

2. From the spiritual gifts listed in this chapter, which ones do you believe you have? How can you use them to "increase (or build up) the body (of Christ)"?

3. What are some ministry needs your church can meet?

8

Evangelize the Sinner:

New Testament Strategy of Evangelism— Program and Plan

Christ is the Head of the church, His Body. When He is lifted up, His life permeates the body with vitality. The saints within the church are equipped through the fellowship of the Christ-life within the body.

Evangelism is the natural result of a Christ-filled body, alive and functioning within a community. Evangelism is not an event, a meeting, or an activity. It may include all of these, but evangelism is more. Evangelism is the outflow of the overflow of the Christ-life in a church body.

Jesus set forth the New Testament strategy of evangelism in the closing chapters of each of the Gospels and in Acts 1:8. It is a strategy of perennial, life-style evangelism.

Last words are important words. The last words of a dying loved one, the last words of one about to depart, make deep impressions. They are carefully weighed words. They are words that give direction; they motivate, challenge, and keep one on course. The last words of Jesus before He left His church to go back to the Father are like that. They are words of mission.

Strategy of Evangelism
Set Forth in Scripture

All power is given unto me in heaven and in earth. Go ye therefore, and teach all nations, baptizing them in the name of the Father, and of the Son, and of the Holy Ghost: Teaching them to observe all things whatsoever I have commanded you: and, lo, I am with you always, even unto the end of the world (Matt. 28:18-20).

These verses are called the Great Commission. They include a four-step cycle in reaching the world for Christ.

"Go." The world can only be reached by going. The church cannot remain in its little cluster of safety and reach its world.

"Teach all nations." The *New International Version* has it, "Make disciples." Making disciples includes winning people to Jesus and leading them to follow Christ.

"Baptizing them in the name of the Father, and of the Son, and of the Holy Ghost." The commitment of those who are won to Christ is crystallized through an open profession of faith in baptism. Baptism is the initial outward witness of the experience a person has had with Christ.

"Teaching them to observe all things whatsoever I have commanded you." The convert must be taught the commands of our Lord and be led into a joyful spirit of obedience to those commands. One of His primary commands is to "Go and make disciples."

Hence, the cycle is back to the beginning. If obeyed, the Commission results in an ever-enlarging circle of witness. The presence of Jesus is assured as one obeys His commission.

Whatever is needed for God's people to fulfill the mission of Jesus, He promises to supply.

> Thus it is written, and thus it behooved Christ to suffer, and to rise from the dead the third day: And that repentance and remission of sins should be preached in his name among all nations, beginning at Jerusalem. And ye are witnesses of these things (Luke 24:46-48).

The message for world evangelization is the death and resurrection of our Lord Jesus Christ. The mission is to call people of all nations to come to Christ through repentance from sin.

> Peace be unto you: as my Father hath sent me, even so send I you. And when he had said this, he breathed on them, and saith unto them, Receive ye the Holy Ghost: Whosesoever sins ye remit, they are remitted unto them; and whose soever sins ye retain, they are retained (John 20:21-23).

The disciples of Jesus are agents of redemption. When Spirit-filled witnesses reach out with the gospel of forgiveness, people will respond and be forgiven. When the church disobediently withholds the good news of forgiveness, people will remain in their sins.

> But ye shall receive power, after that the Holy Ghost is come upon you: and ye shall be witnesses unto me both in Jerusalem, and in all Judea, and in Samaria, and unto the uttermost part of the earth (Acts 1:8).

In Acts 1:8, Jesus gives the methodology for reaching the world. He had already given the message. Motivation for accomplishing the mission He gives in a twofold way: first, through His teachings; second, through the Holy Spirit that would come at Pentecost. Then He set forth New Testament methodology for world evangelization.[1]

The little band of followers was small. Written across the entire situation would have been the word *impossible!* But because they did what He said, we are Christians on the other side of the earth today. His strategy has not changed.[2] It can be summarized in two words: *go tell.*

Dr. Roy Fish, professor of evangelism at Southwestern Baptist Theological Seminary in Fort Worth, Texas, has stated that today we are guilty of a subtle reversal of the New Testament strategy. We are engaging in a "come hear" strategy of evangelism. We invite people to Sunday School to "come hear" the teacher teach. We invite people to church services to "come hear" the preacher preach. Inviting people to Sunday School, to church, and to revival meetings should not be ceased. But inviting people to church will never reach our world for Christ.

Gil Stricklin, former director of personal evangelism for the Baptist General Convention of Texas, humorously remarked that inviting people to church is like "making an appointment between a fish and a fisherman."

Jesus said, "Follow me, and I will make you fishers of men" (Matt 4:19). The methodology of Jesus in reaching our world involves four things (Acts 1:8):

A Priority—"Witnesses unto me."

A Plan—"In Jerusalem, and in all Judea, and in Samaria, and unto the uttermost part of the earth."

Personnel—"Ye shall be."

Power—"Ye shall receive power, after that the Holy Ghost is come upon you."

The Priority of Evangelization ("Witnesses unto Me")

"Witnesses unto me." The program of the church is to witness unto Jesus. Every activity and program of the church must point people to Jesus.

A multitude of things go on in the life of any church. Preachers preach, teachers teach, choirs sing, buildings are built, budgets are subscribed, but the priority of the church is to witness unto Jesus. All else is for naught if the church is not witnessing unto Jesus. The danger for church members is that they become so involved in a multitude of activities that they cease to witness. If a man's being a deacon gets in the way of his witnessing, he needs to resign the deaconship. He needs to get back to the priority of being a witness that Christ has for him to be. A deacon cannot be the church leader he needs to be unless he is a faithful, consistent witness.

Teachers must be witnesses. They are not simply to prepare a Bible lesson to present to a class. The teacher is responsible for reaching people, leading them in an understanding of God's Word and in winning them to Jesus Christ. The Sunday School needs teachers who are soulwinners.

Nothing fills a choir with a dynamic of joy and power like personal witnessing. The finest voices may sing in a church choir, but the sounds may be empty and hollow. Nothing gives more power to the singing of a choir than for members to have witnessed for Christ and see in the congregation those they have led to the Lord. As the invitation is given, what a thrill it is for a choir member to see the one to whom she has witnessed come forward confessing Christ as Savior.

No preacher can preach with continuous effectiveness unless he personally shares Christ with people day by day on a life-style basis. His words become simply a lecture or an oration.

Since witnessing is so important, some have concluded that it is tremendously difficult. But witnessing is the natural expression of a Christian. A witness denotes one who can or does tell what he has seen or heard or knows.

On a New Year's Eve night, our church was having an extended Watch Night service. There was singing, Bible study of the Book of Hosea, and prayer. Charles, an engineer in one of the space-related programs, and his family attended. He said he came that night to church to keep from getting drunk. He had been drunk every New Year's since he could remember.

Charles was captivated by the study of God's Word. He accepted Christ as personal Savior.

The next week I invited him to go with me to another church where I was teaching a Bible study. I wanted to nurture him. On our way I instructed him in how to study the Bible. I shared my observation that God had gifted him with a genuine discernment of the Scripture, and that God would make his life fruitful if he would study the Word, stay humble, and be available.

The second night he came with me again. Again I shared with him, "Charles, the Lord wants you to witness."

Charles asked, "What does that mean?"

We were driving along the freeway. I said, "Suppose suddenly that automobile in front of us crashes into another. You saw what happened. The court subpoenaed you as a witness. What would they ask you to do?"

Charles answered, "I would simply have to tell what I saw and know."

"That is a witness. That is exactly what you do in relationship to Jesus. You tell what you have experienced and know of Christ."

"Oh!" replied Charles excitedly, "I have already been doing that. I've been telling people at work what Jesus has done in my life. They are interested!"

Witnessing is telling others what we have experienced and know of Jesus. Witnessing is the program of the church! The object of our witness is Jesus. The witness does not call attention to himself. He does not simply invite people to church. He shares Jesus. There is authority and power in the very name of Jesus.

Persons can be neutral about religion, church, and even about God. But it is impossible to be neutral about Jesus. We are with Him or against Him.

As we share Jesus, conviction comes. One Thursday night, a witnessing team from our church knocked on the door of Jerry and Linda. The team included my wife, Kathy, JoAnn, a young lady who worked for a financial institution, and Sam, our city manager.

Sam had recently recommitted his life to Christ. He had been a carnal Christian. He had sat in the balcony looking at his watch while I preached. His goal had been to beat the Methodists to the restaurant, finish eating, and get to the golf course before his buddies arrived. One Sunday during the invitation, he all but fell out of the balcony. He was down at the front. He did not know why. God was dealing with him. He recommitted his life to Christ. He became involved in the church. When we had a *WIN School,* Sam participated. At city hall they nicknamed him "Preacher."

JoAnn knocked on the door. She introduced the others.

She said, "We are from First Baptist Church, but we did not come to talk with you about church. We came to share with you about Jesus. May we come in?"

They were pleasantly invited in. JoAnn began to share Christ with Linda. Linda responded that she was a Christian, but she did not go to church.

Jerry interrupted, "I am the reason. I drink. I am not a Christian. I will not let her go."

This gave Sam a good opportunity to share. He told Jerry that he identified with him. Sam said, "It has not been long since I was not living for Christ."

Their witness was so meaningful that Jerry and Linda followed our witnessing team all the way to the automobile.

Thirty minutes after our team had left, Jerry came under conviction. He called his employer who was a Christian. He told his employer that he wanted to be saved that very night. His employer came over and led him to Christ.

The next Sunday, Jerry and Linda were at the altar at First Baptist Church. They confessed Christ and were baptized. That night, Jerry brought his brother and sister-in-law to church. He walked down the aisle with them. He had led them to Christ that afternoon.

In sharing his personal testimony, Jerry told how many people had come to their door asking them to come to church. He said, "We were not interested in church. We would get rid of them the best way we could. We knew how to get rid of Baptists. We would tell them that we were Catholics. They would not come back!

"These people said that they had come to talk with us

about Jesus. We were not interested in church, but we were interested in Jesus," he said.

The name of Jesus is captivating and life changing. The program of the church is witnessing unto Jesus.

The Plan for Evangelization

Jesus' method for world evangelization involves the plan He set forth in Acts 1:8: "In Jerusalem, and in all Judea, and in Samaria, and unto the uttermost part of the earth." The plan was to witness in an ever-extending series of concentric circles. It began in Jerusalem, then went throughout Judaea; then Samaria, the semi-Jewish state, and would be a kind of bridge leading out into the heathen world. Finally, this witness was to go to the ends of the earth.

Jesus' plan was then and is now to use His people to win the world to Himself. They were to saturate their city with the gospel, to confront each person with the claims of Christ on his life.

Total Penetration

Jesus set forth the strategy of total evangelism. That is, the penetration of the entire world with the gospel of Christ. It involved the church in confronting every person with the claims of Christ upon their lives in that generation.[3]

The early church did what Jesus commanded. The Book of Acts records the history of the spreading of the gospel. It followed the pattern of Jesus' command in Acts 1:8.

The mission of Jesus for the church today has not changed. His strategy is still total penetration of our world by the church with His gospel in this generation. The question is: "How is this strategy applied by a local church in the modern world?"

Define a Geographic Area

Each local church should define a definite geographic area or areas. The church accepts the responsibility of confronting every person in that area, personally, with the gospel of Christ in the power of the Holy Spirit.

The following is a step-by-step procedure:

(1) Locate the church building on a map of its community.

(2) Estimate the radius of influence of the church. Extend a radius line on the map in each direction. The lines may extend as far out as the majority of the church's members live.

(3) Draw a circle around that area. Consider it as the primary area of witness for the church in beginning its penetration.

(4) Saturate the primary area with the gospel. Confront every person in that circle with the claims of Christ on his life. Begin with the people in the house next door to the church building. Continue to extend the witness out from the place of beginning.

(5) The circle of primary influence will become an ever enlarging circle.[4]

(6) Churches in the same general area will have overlapping circles of influence. This is positive. Their witness is not that of competition. It is complementary. If every church is doing the same thing, the witness will be powerful. It will create a consciousness of the Lord in that area. A climate for evangelism will develop where people will come under deep conviction.

The following pages will illustrate the procedure (see diagram 9.1).

Two levels of penetration are saturation and confrontation. General saturation creates an openness for the gospel. Prospects are discovered. They receive a witness. Interest develops. But relatively few will be saved through saturation alone.

Confronting individuals in a one-on-one witnessing situation is necessary if many people are to be led to Christ. Like the Ethiopian who was confronted by Philip in the desert,

Diagram 8.1

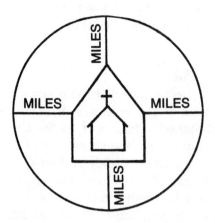

Overlapping circles of influence of several local churches

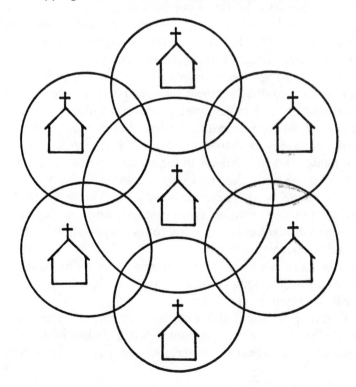

they need "someone to guide them." A Home Mission Board PROBE or LASER are effective saturation tools. Contact the Church Extension section for more information.

Saturation

Plan for saturation.

(1) Use general broadcasting of the gospel seed. Thoroughly sow the field of the church's primary area so that every person is touched with a witness for Christ.

(2) Make a periodic contact with every residence. At least once every six months, every resident should have a personal visit, receive a gospel tract and information about the church, or receive a telephone call.

(3) Publicize events, programs, studies, and aspects of the church life that will appeal to a need of unreached persons of the community. Publicize consistently.

(4) Utilize all available means of spreading the word about Jesus and the church. Use the newspaper, newcomer packets, signs, billboards, radio, television, printed material distributed through businesses, public places, and members. Use door-to-door witness surveys periodically for witness saturation and to discover prospects. Build a prospect file for continuing follow-up. Utilize direct mail and telephoning to gain access to every home in the area.

One pastor led his church to focus one-on-one within the church's larger area that had been targeted for saturation. They are covering the area zone by zone. During a three-month period they mailed two postcards and one letter to each of the households. The mailouts were followed by a door-to-door witness survey.

Results were positive. Many prospects were discovered. Some made professions of faith. Only one slightly negative response was reported.

(5) Conduct evangelistic events periodically that will draw out "seekers" from the community. Utilize evangelistic crusades, special music programs, one-night evangelistic

services, special speakers, evangelistic banquets and dinners, and testimonies.

Confrontation

Prepare for confrontation. Personal confrontation of every individual with the claims of Christ is the mission of a local church.

Total Participation

What is the mission of a local church? *Our mission is to discover every person for whom we are responsible and to minister to him or her at the point of that person's deepest need.* This definition was the outgrowth of my realization of a need in the church that I pastored for a unity in understanding of the church's primary mission. It is Jesus centered and people centered. Its emphasis is on people reaching people. Let us analyze the definition phrase by phrase.

"Every person": We are not much concerned about people we do not know. A burden comes as we begin to individualize our concern and relate it to specific persons. *People are reached and discipled one by one, not by masses.*

"Discover every person": We do not reach many people we do not know. The first step toward reaching people is to discover them and to get to know them. Place their names and information about them in the church's evangelism prospect file.

We do not discover people who need Jesus by attending church services. Gathering to worship is precious and right. It is commanded by God. But if we are to discover the multitudes who are lost, we must go where they are, and they are not in church.

Where do we find the lost?

Behind doors—in the houses and apartments of our community. We must knock on their doors.

Behind labels—many wear religious labels. It is socially acceptable to wear a religious label of some sort—Baptist,

Methodist, Catholic, Hindu, Moslem, Jehovah's Witness, and so forth. It is popular to be religious. But many of those who wear labels are lost.

A religious label can mean any number of things. A person may claim the Baptist label simply because she attended that church once. Or she might have thought about attending that church. Or her grandparents might have gone to that church. It may be simply a religious preference.

Behind masks of happy faces may hide empty lives. There are masks of financial security, masks of worldly enjoyment, and masks of busy activity that hide a seeking heart within lonely meaningless existence.

Behind barriers—racial, social, language, and economic barriers. Some persons are behind prison walls. Some are in hospitals and other institutions. Some are behind social barriers that many Christians feel threatened to penetrate. Some are behind economic barriers of wealth or poverty. Some of the most spiritually neglected people in our world are the wealthy and worldly successful. Everywhere we go, we find lost people.

How do we find the lost?

We find them through door-to-door surveys conducted periodically in the neighborhood of the church area, through telephone surveys covering every listing in the directory, and through visitors who attend the worship services at church meetings.

A visitor attends for a reason. Every visitor should be followed up with a visit or phone call to determine whether or not he had a need to which the church should minister. Three types of contacts should be made to every visitor: contact by letter, contact by phone, and contact by personal visit.

We find lost people through members of the church submitting "lost friend" and "unenlisted friend" names.

We find them through bus ministry, both saturation and confrontation happens.

We find lost people through new members, especially new converts. Every new convert has a circle of influence. She has many acquaintances who are lost or unenlisted. She should be encouraged to witness to them. The church should assist her in witnessing to them. Many new members have family members who are lost. Follow-up on them should be consistent.

We find lost people through involvement with people in the daily activities of life, for example at weddings, funerals, PTA meetings, ball games, businesses, stores, and so forth.

"For whom we are responsible": We are responsible to minister to every person who is lost and/or who is not actively involved in the life of another church.

"To minister to him or her at the point of that person's deepest need": The church is to minister to people at the point of their need (Matt. 25:35-45). Often, in order to reach through to the deepest need, we must begin by meeting a surface need. By providing shoes for children's feet, food for the table, for counseling to help with life's problems, an opening is provided to reach through to the deeper need of the spiritual life. However, if the church only provides shoes, clothes, and counsel, and does not lead people to Christ, it is no different from welfare agencies and social clubs.

We have noted the definition of the mission of the church. Now let us examine the designation of prospects for the church's ministry.

Who Is a Prospect?

Every person we meet is a prospect for our witness. He is not necessarily a prospect for our church, but for our witness. You cannot witness to the wrong person. Every person you meet is either saved or lost. If he is saved and receives our witness, he will rejoice with us in Christ. We have found

a new brother. As I went through customs in Korea, I hand-
ed an official a Billy Graham booklet, *Steps to Peace with
God.* I said, "May I share with you this good news about
Jesus Christ? Billy Graham wrote this booklet." (Billy Graham had been to Korea. Many people in Seoul had heard
him.)

The customs official quickly said in English, "I am a
Christian, too." His face lightened with a broad smile as he
extended a brotherly handshake. The first person I met on
the other side of the earth was a brother. What a joy that
was! If we witness to a person and find that he is saved, we
can rejoice together in Christ.

If the person is lost, she needs our witness. She may not
respond immediately, or her response may even be negative. Still, she needs our witness. The Holy Spirit will use
the witness in a way that we may never know.

D. L. Moody once said, "I see every person as though he
had a huge 'L' in the midst of his forehead. I consider him
lost until I know he is saved."

Every non-Christian and every inactive Christian is a
prospect for our ministry. As we minister to him at the point
of his need, he will be stirred to commitment. As he follows
Christ he will either go to his own church, go to another
church, or come to our church. The church to which the
Lord leads a person is secondary. The primary thing is that
the person commits his life to Christ and follows Him.

As a church totally penetrates its community, a God consciousness is created. The Holy Spirit works through the
Word to convict hearts. People begin to think *God.* As persons begin to think *God*, they become open to the witness of
a believer. They begin to reach out, seeking God.

The principle of penetration is a confidence builder for
witnessing. The Lord who set forth this strategy knows human nature. In the light of that nature, He set forth His
strategy to reach humanity. We are not alone in our efforts

and attempts to reach people. God cares more about them than we do.

Regardless of who it is, sooner or later every person in your community will think *God.* Whether he is an atheist, skeptic, immoral, or indifferent, he will sooner or later think *God.*

God loves that person so much that He will allow circumstances to come that the person cannot handle alone. Every person eventually will face a brick wall in his life. When he comes to the end of himself, he will think *God.*

When he thinks *God,* we want him to think of our church. We want him to think *that church is where I can find out about God* because it has not been long since someone from our church touched his or her life in a positive way for Jesus.

Jesus' plan of penetration is universal. As our church began to apply this strategy, some of our people knocked on the door of a family just two blocks from the church building. These people did not even know the church building existed. They drove by it every day but did not know what it was. The husband was a musician in a dance band. The wife was an alcoholic.

Our people shared Christ with this couple. Before long, family problems surfaced. They reached out to the church because someone had touched their lives in a positive way. One of our people led them to Christ. Today, both are actively committed Christians. Now the musician plays and sings for the glory of Christ.

A few blocks away lived an old man who was dying of throat cancer. He would have never responded to a "come hear" strategy. Our people were practicing the "go tell" strategy of penetration when two of our ladies knocked on his door. They led him to Christ. They returned to nurture him in Christ. He requested baptism. The only time he was able to attend church was for his baptism. In a few weeks, his life was gone.

Glory fills the lives of individuals and of a church when Jesus' plan of penetration is practiced.

Evangelism Techniques in the Early Church

Establishing an evangelistic church growth strategy can be powerfully implemented by following the principles of a balance in evangelistic techniques. The early church blended together the following five basic techniques to fulfill the strategy of total evangelism:

1. Public Proclamation
2. Caring Affirmation and Ministry
3. Event Attraction
4. Geographic Saturation
5. Personal Presentation

These evangelism techniques, if practiced biblically by a local church, will result in mighty power and maximum penetration for evangelism.

Public Proclamation

The preaching and teaching of the gospel publicly majors on an appeal to the lost to accept Christ and follow Him in baptism and committed living. Biblical models are the powerful preaching and teaching of the apostles and laity. Peter in Acts 2, Stephen in Acts 7, and Paul in Acts 22 are examples.

Effective evangelistic proclamation today is being done by many pastors in worship services and other meetings. It is also being done by many preachers in revivals and crusades and by many Sunday School teachers in classrooms. An evangelistic Sunday School is a mighty force for reaching and equipping people for Christ. It must be staffed with directors, teachers, and workers who not only teach the word of God and build a caring fellowship, but who are also committed to reaching people and leading them to Christ. A Sunday School class can be an effective soul-winning team.

Three ingredients must be present in effective proclamation evangelism. First, lost people must be present to be affected by proclamation. Jesus went out where the people were and proclaimed the good news. If we reach the lost today through preaching and teaching, we must either go where they are or attract them to our meetings. Not only must the lost be present, they must be able to understand the message. Second, the gospel and how to be saved must be clearly presented. Third, an effective invitation must be extended. The invitation or appeal should be marked by urgency, clarity, integrity, and compassion. Every preacher should learn how to give an effective invitation. The invitation should be planned carefully and made an object of prayer, not something simply tacked on to the end of a sermon.

Caring Affirmation

Caring affirmation happens when the upright, godly, caring lives of the people of God touch the lost. It involves Christians in caring and ministering to lost people so that a door is opened to present the gospel and to lead them to Christ.

The people were so impressed by what they saw on the day of Pentecost that they asked, "What meaneth this?" (Acts 2:12). Verse 47 indicates that Christians had favor with all the people. Acts 4:13: "Now when they saw the boldness of Peter and John, and perceived that they were unlearned and ignorant men, they marveled; and they took knowledge of them, that they had been with Jesus. " Dorcas in Acts 9 made a tremendous impact on the entire area of Joppa through her loving ministry to the widows.

Today Christians can effectively reach people through establishing witnessing relationships; counseling; giving encouraging support; caring for the sick; providing food, clothing, and shelter for the needy; visiting the lonely in homes, institutions, nursing homes; and countless other possibilities. Caring ministry affirms gospel witness. It opens the door for Christians to lead people to new life in Christ. However, upright living and ministry that does not present Christ will reach few people for Christ. If we feed the hungry, clothe and house the poor, and minister to many but do not share Jesus with them, the church becomes no different from a social or government welfare agency.

The mission of the church is to share Christ with every person at the point of his or her deepest need. The deepest need of every person is spiritual. Often in order to reach to the deepest need, we begin with people's surface need by putting shoes on their feet, clothes on their back, or giving counsel and assistance to help in their trouble. But let us never stop until we have shared Christ with them to meet the deepest need of their spiritual lives. Multitudes in America can be reached for Christ through the caring affirmation of churches ministering in the name of Christ. A challenging example is a relatively small church in Arkansas that baptized 130 in one year through a Job Corps ministry. It assisted hundred in locating jobs, shared Christ with them, and discipled them. Needs-based small groups are very effective in developing evangelistic ministry. Needs-based small groups differ from Bible-based small groups in Sunday School.

Event Attraction

This is the third evangelistic technique in the early chapters of Acts. It involved believers in presenting the gospel to people who were attracted through the mighty works of God in their midst.

In Acts 3 the lame man at the Beautiful Gate was healed and went leaping and praising God through the temple. A great crowd was attracted. Peter preached to them. Acts 4:4

notes, "Howbeit many of them which heard the word believed; and the number of the men was about five thousand."

The attraction technique can legitimately be used by churches today. Events will attract people who would not be open to the regular services of the church. Messages and testimonies of Christians in whose lives God has done a mighty work will attract the lost. Special music programs will attract others. Speakers on subjects that focus on "felt needs" of people will attract others. These are only a few of the event attractions that can be utilized to reach people.

Attracting the lost and unchurched to special events provides two advantages to a church. First, the gospel may be presented, and some will be saved immediately. Second, the names and addresses of those not making decisions may be secured for follow-up visits of witness and ministry. It is important that follow-up contacts be made soon after a person attends an event.

There is, however, a danger in event attraction. It is possible for a church to go too far in depending on events to reach people. Churches may also resort to sensationalism, depending on superficial and even unworthy and worldly activities to attract a crowd. Event attraction must be kept in balance in the church's ministry. Then, it provides a dynamic to the church life that helps to reach people for Christ. It becomes a part of a church's total evangelistic thrust.

Geographic Saturation

The fourth evangelistic technique practiced by the early church is *geographic saturation*. The believers in Ephesus saturated the geographic area of Asia so that within two years "all they which dwelt in Asia heard the word of the Lord Jesus, both Jews and Greeks" (Acts 19:10b).

From Jerusalem the believers were "scattered abroad throughout the regions of Judea and Samaria, except the apostles" (8:1). The occasion God used for spreading the gospel was the great persecution that arose from the stoning of Stephen. Acts 8:4 says, "Therefore they that were scattered abroad went every where preaching the word." The word for "preach" is the Greek word *euangelidzomenoi (evangelizing)*. The word indicates that they "announced the good news, gossiped, chattered about, and shared about" Jesus everywhere they went. All of the believers were evangelizing. They saturated the entire area with the gospel.

In present-day application a church will identify a geographic area and periodically saturate it with the gospel and with information about the church. Every member can be involved in some way to get the word of Jesus to every person in the area. Various methods need to be employed. Some of these are listed on pages 176-183. The church's goal should be to discover every prospect, include the information in its permanent prospect file or prospect computer list, and share Christ with that person.

Saturation alone will not lead many people to Christ and into the church. But without saturation not many will be reached. It creates a climate for evangelism. It increases the God-consciousness in a community. It recognizes the harvest principle of evangelism. If there is to be a harvest, much seed-sowing must be done. Saturation is the general broadcasting of the gospel "seed" in an area. If we sow sparingly we will reap sparingly. If we sow bountifully, a bountiful harvest can be reaped. Many churches attempt to reap a harvest where little seed sowing has been done. Thus, relatively few people are reached. Geographic saturation is essential to the strategy of total evangelism.

For the first four techniques to result in maximum fruitfulness of reaching people, the fifth technique is absolutely necessary. People come to Christ one by one. Many must be personally guided through the conversion experience. If personal soul-winning is neglected though a church may implement the first four techniques, it will result in a much lower percentage of people saved and baptized.

Personal Presentation of the Gospel

Personal presentation of the gospel of Christ is the fifth technique of reaching the lost. It is the spiritually sensitive confrontation of an individual with the claims of Christ on his or her life. It involves a caring believer guiding a lost person through the conversion experience under the leadership of the Holy Spirit.

Personal confrontation is illustrated in the story of Philip and the Eunuch in Acts 8. Philip was led by the Spirit to leave his successful revival campaign in Samaria to go down to the desert. His path crossed the path of the Ethiopian caravan at just the point where he observed the Ethiopian treasurer of Queen Candace. The Eunuch was reading from a scroll of Isaiah. Perhaps he was a product of the first four techniques of evangelism. He had been to Jerusalem where he had heard public proclamation, felt the caring affirmation of the disciples, been attracted by the mighty works of God, and was a product of saturation. He had a copy of the Scripture and was reading it, but he was not yet saved. Philip was spiritually sensitive. He drew near the chariot and asked, "Understand thou what thou readest?" And he said, "How can I, except some man should guide me?" Philip began there and guided him through the conversion experience. The man believed and requested baptism. Tradition has it that the man went home and began the great Ethiopian church that continues to this day.

Multitudes can be reached for Christ as believers are equipped for soul-winning. It should be the goal of every pastor to inspire and equip every member in leading people to come to Christ and in guiding them tenderly through the conversion experience and into the life of the church. For maximum effectiveness and fruitfulness in reaching its community for Christ, a church should incorporate each of the five techniques of balanced evangelism. Churches have access to support, resource materials, and people through their state evangelism director and through the Evangelism Section of the Home Mission Board.

Questions

1. Respond to the statement: "Every activity and program of the church must point people to Jesus." Are there any programs in your church that do not point people to Jesus?

2. If you were going to saturate a two-mile radius from your church with the gospel, what kinds of activities would you do?

3. What do the phrases *total penetration* and *total participation* mean to you?

9   Evangelize the Sinner:

New Testament Strategy of Evangelism— Personnel and Power

Personnel for Evangelization (Acts 1:8)

"Ye shall be witnesses unto me" (Acts 1:8).

Each church has adequate personnel to evangelize its community. The personnel are those in the pews every Sunday. *You* in Acts 1:8 is plural. Jesus is speaking to the entire membership of the church. His call to every Christian is to witness. By virtue of who you are in Christ, by virtue of who Christ is in you—you *are* His witness. There is no choice. We have no option. Every Christian is a witness unto Jesus. The only choice is to obey or disobey. A Christian may be a disobedient witness or an obedient witness. His witness may be negative or positive, but he is a witness.

Total penetration of our world with the gospel demands *total participation* of the membership of the church in witnessing. For too long the laity has attended meetings, given money, and prayed, while depending on paid preachers and church staffs to do the witnessing. According to a recent survey, it requires one thousand laypersons and six ministers one year to lead one person to Christ.[1]

It is tragic that 95 percent of the Christians today never lead a soul to Christ. This is the reversal of Jesus' strategy of New Testament evangelism. These trends must change if our world is to be reached.

The hope for reaching our world with the gospel is to harness the tremendous resources available to the church. Every church has an army of laypeople with a potential witnessing power to penetrate its community.

No matter how well educated, how capable of communication, how gifted, or how committed our preachers may be, the people of our world will never be reached from pulpits of our churches. These people are not coming to church. The church must go to them.[2]

It would be unnatural for masses of lost people to come to church. It would be against their nature. The most uncomfortable place for a lost person to be is in church. There the Holy Spirit moves with convicting power. The lost person feels like an outsider.

While we need to continue to invite people to church, primarily the church must reach people where they are. Preachers and church leaders cannot do this alone. There are not enough of them. Not enough time is available for them to confront every person in the area of their particular church with the gospel. To do this, the church must marshal its great army of laypeople for witness. Besides, if preachers could do it alone, it would rob the laity of the greatest joy in service they can know. The personnel for reaching our world for Jesus are laypeople. Jesus calls every Christian to witness.

A church and its leaders have a responsibility to God to involve its great army of laity in witness for Jesus Christ. Four steps are necessary in doing so.

Enlighten the Laity

Many Christians do not witness because they do not realize that they are supposed to witness. They think witnessing is the job of the preachers. It is a spiritual work; they do not feel spiritual.

The church must preach, teach, and instruct the laity in truth about the role of the layperson in the life of the New

Testament church. The laity must realize that witnessing is not an option. Jesus gave no choice. Witnessing is His mandate.

Enlist the Laity

Laypeople are enlisted for every task under the sun. But all too often the church makes no effort to enlist them for witnessing. A church must establish its priorities to make witnessing and soul-winning its basic program. Unless it does, laypeople will be enlisted in so many committees, activities, social functions, service projects, recreational events that they have no time left to participate in witnessing through the organized church program. Then they will have no incentive to practice life-style witnessing daily.

Laypeople are at different levels of spiritual maturity. They need to be involved at some level of outreach. Every layperson can be involved in some way. Beginning involvement may be in doing surveys, distributing tracts, door-to-door Bible or literature distribution, and so forth.

As people are enlisted and involved in some project of outreach, they will be more likely to participate in witness-training preparation. It should be the goal of the church to enlist every layperson in its organized equipping program for witnessing and soul-winning.

Equip the Laity

Many laypeople have a deep longing to witness. But they do not know how. This fact is well illustrated by the lay leadership in a church I once pastored. I had recently accepted the pastorate in that church. We studied the New Testament strategy of evangelism. We studied Jesus' plan for saturating our city with the gospel and confronting every individual with the claims of Christ on his or her life.

I shared with the leadership of the church that as pastor I could not accomplish His plan alone. I asked them to commit their lives to Christ for personal witnessing. Then I asked them to allow me to equip them to assist me in equipping the laypeople of our church. The group I challenged included the Sunday School director, Discipleship Training director, chairman of deacons, Women's Missionary Union director, Brotherhood director, treasurer, and others. They all responded positively but with some anxiety.

The WMU director was an excellent leader. She carried out her WMU duties effectively. What she said indicated her commitment but, also, her anxiety.

"Pastor, I will come to the *WIN Lay Evangelism School.* I will come to the *WIN Lay Evangelism Teacher Training School.* I will learn how to teach our women to witness. But you must know this. I cannot witness myself. I have tried and failed. But I will learn how to teach others."

I replied, "That is fine. I am glad that you will do that." (I felt that I knew what would happen if she participated in the *WIN Lay Evangelism School.*)

When the teams went out to witness during the Lay Evangelism School, our WMU director did participate. But she did not have the opportunity to witness to anyone. However, God had done a work in her life. God had spoken to her heart about her beautician, Cookie. At the beauty shop she sat under her hair dryer thumbing through her witness booklet. She hoped Cookie would ask what she was reading.

Finally, Cookie asked, "What are you reading?"

She said, "I'm reading a little booklet about Jesus. May I share it with you?"

They read through the booklet together. Cookie was very interested. When they came to the suggested prayer in the booklet. Cookie was ready to pray and be saved.

Our WMU director panicked. She walked out. She left Cookie high and dry. She came rushing tearfully to the church office to see the pastor.

These were her words to me, "Pastor, Cookie is ready to be saved. You have got to go save her!"

This is the response of many laypeople to soul-winning opportunities. When someone is ready to be saved, they come to tell the preacher. The preacher can "draw the net."

I was determined that I would equip our WMU director to lead people to Christ. I said, "Yes, I will go, if you will go with me."

We made an appointment for our Brotherhood director, WMU director, and myself to visit Cookie and her husband. We were there no more than thirty minutes when both of them accepted Christ. At that point, Cookie said something to our WMU director that broke her heart and changed her life.

Cookie said, "You have invited me to church. You have invited me to Sunday School. You have asked me to come hear your preacher preach. But you have never told me before about Jesus! Why?"

At that moment our WMU director made a commitment to tell people about Christ. Later she went back and led Cookie's son to the Lord. Then she visited Cookie's aging mother and led her to Christ. Soon, she led a neighbor to the Lord, then her own father. Since that time, she has continued consistently to lead people to Christ.

As she gave her testimony about beginning to witness, she shared some things with which many people will identify. She said there were three reasons she did not witness.

"First, I did not witness because I did not think God expected that of me. I thought witnessing was for special people. I thought this was for preachers, evangelists, and others like them. But, I came to realize that every Christian, including myself, is to be a witness for Jesus.

"Second, I did not witness because I did not think I had a testimony. I was saved when I was fourteen years old . I did not have a sensational testimony. No one would be interested in what happened to me. But I realized that God would use my witness if I pointed people to Jesus.

"Third, I did not witness because I really did not know

how. I was ashamed to admit this. My pride kept me from it. I was WMU director. I had served in many leadership positions in the church. But God dealt with me. I yielded my life to Him to be available as a witness."

Many of our people do not witness for those same reasons. They must be enlightened, enlisted, equipped, and engaged in witness for our Lord. The pastor must make it a priority to equip laypeople to share Christ. Pastors must do so by instruction. They must teach Jesus' strategy and methods from the Scriptures.

Pastors must do so by example. On-the-job training is an effective method of equipping for witness. Pastors should take laypeople with them to show them how to do it.

As laypeople are equipped, they in turn equip others. The lay leaders I mentioned, and others, gave themselves to equip Christians in their organizations to share Christ.

One layman retired from his position as a university professor to give himself full-time to the ministry of winning others and equipping others to lead people to Christ. He has been used extensively in his own church and in many other churches in the equipping ministry.

WIN School: A Lay Evangelism Strategy, One-Day Soul-Winning Seminars, Continuing Witness Training, Building Witnessing Relationships, People Sharing Jesus, Life-style Witnessing for Women, and other witness and soul-winning seminars, personal witnessing rallies, and so forth should be conducted periodically to train people in witness. Training events and schools, however, are not adequate alone. A continuous week-by-week practice and instruction needs to be a part of the church's regular program.

We set aside one day each week for witness training and visitation. Witness teams can be developed. An experienced witness is teamed with one or two less-experienced ones to equip them.

One of the best methods of *discipling* Christians is to involve them in witnessing. A commitment to witness consistently will drive one to prayer, create a desire for Bible study, and force one to give attention to personal daily conduct.

Gear the church to equip the laity to share Christ. If this is done, there will be perennial revival.

Engage the Laity

Every church has a corporate witness within the community. The life of the body influences the spiritual, moral, social, and economic life of its community.

"Ye are the salt of the earth.. . . Ye are the light of the world" (Matt. 5:13-14).

Many churches have lost their witness and influence through sin, divisiveness, lovelessness, church fights, and so forth. Often an individual believer who is witnessing in the community of such a church must apologize for the church's behavior. A church must keep its witness strong and pure as a body. This gives support and strength to the personal witness of the believer.[3]

Personal witness is primary. There is no other way many individuals will be won to Christ. Many never attend church to hear the gospel. They never have a contact with the preacher. The laity has opportunity to share Jesus with them. There is no other way many will ever be confronted with the gospel except through the personal witness of a believer.

Personal witnessing develops a sensitivity to people. It causes Christians to see every person they meet as a person God loves. People come to realize that they are responsible to share Jesus with others.

Preparation is necessary for personal witnessing to be effective. Careful preparation must be made by the church and by individuals.

Spiritual preparation is required.—Witnessing is a spiritual work. It must be done in the power of the Holy Spirit. Prayer, cleansing from sin, and the fullness of the Holy Spirit are preparation for witness.

Personal preparation is required.—Physical, mental, and emotional preparation must be made by the individual witness.

Formal preparation is needed.—Doctrinal and procedural studies should be used. WIN Lay Evangelism Schools, soul-winning, witnessing, and discipleship courses are profitable.

Supervised preparation is helpful.—Use of on-the-job training techniques is an asset. A beginning witness learns from a more experienced one.

Continuous preparation is necessary.—One never learns enough about Jesus, the Bible, the work of the Holy Spirit, and the nature of humanity to make personal preparation complete. If you stop preparing, you grow stale. What you have learned and practiced becomes vague and ineffective. You must continue to prepare.

Simultaneous preparation is essential.—A person must be involved in witness as she prepares. If not, preparation is meaningless. People who plan to wait until they are fully prepared to start witnessing seldom do.

You must tell what you know. This is obedience to Jesus' commission. If you will, the Holy Spirit will use the feeblest witness to accomplish great things. *It is not our ability but our availability* that God blesses and uses. Use what you are learning as you learn it.

There are two levels of participation in personal witness in any church. This first is participation in the organized-witness program. Second is participation in life-style witness.

1. Organized-witness program

This disciplines you to be committed to a definite time. It is easy to slip into poor spiritual habits of never or seldom witnessing unless you are committed to an organized, definite witness time. It ensures that someone who might be overlooked otherwise does receive a witness.

It provides a means of being equipped or of equipping others as one witness is teamed with another for visitation.

2. Life-style witness

A goal for every Christian should be to share Christ with people wherever and whenever one meets them. Share with neighbors, relatives, people at work, school, wherever you go.

Organized-witness programs will be minimally effective unless you are a consistent life-style witness.

Far more life-style witnessing goes on in a live church than it does through organized witnessing.

Power for Evangelization

The power of the Holy Spirit is given for witness. "But ye shall receive power, after that the Holy Ghost is come upon you: and ye shall be witnesses unto me" (Acts 1:8).

While there is abundant joy associated with presence of the power of the Holy Spirit, it is not given for our enjoyment. Holy Spirit power is for our employment! It is not given to accomplish human goals. It is given to bring people to Jesus.

The power of the Holy Spirit is given to enable the believer to live the Christ-life. No one but Jesus can live the Jesus-life. The only possibility for a person to live the Christ-life is for Jesus to live His life through the life of the believer. Living the life is foundation for personal witness.

The Holy Spirit equips the witness to verbally share Jesus Christ with others. Apart from Holy Spirit power, the presentation of the gospel is accompanied by a dreadfulness that kills. It is the Spirit who "makes alive."[4] The flow of Holy Spirit power through the life of a church and an individual is directly proportional to obedience in witness.

Where witnessing is minimized, there is little evidence of the power of the Holy Spirit.

A church is permeated with the power of His presence as it faithfully witnesses in obedience to Jesus' commission. Perpetual disobedience to the basic command of our Lord Jesus Christ results in spiritual deadness. It is little wonder that we see such powerlessness within churches when 95 percent of the members live in continuous disobedience to the primary command of Christ.

Power invades the life of an individual as he becomes faithful in life-style witness. Henry is seventy-five years of age. At one time, he was a faithful witness. Then he drifted into a formally religious, self-centered way of life.

Our church began to emphasize personal witnessing. Henry participated in lay evangelism studies and witnessing. One day he led three people to Christ as he visited in the hospital. He said to his pastor, "Thank you for leading us to witness. I had lost my first love. I was miserable. But now I have got back my first love. I am doing again the first work!"

Some continue to pray, "Oh, Lord fill me, give me the power of the Holy Spirit." In answer to some prayers like that God must say, "What for? What would you do with it if I gave it to you? I have already given you more power than you are using now. You are living in disobedience to the very thing for which I have given you power."

Holy Spirit power is available for witness. We are not waiting for Him to come. He is here already. Some who pray for the Holy Spirit to come, pray amiss. We are not waiting for another Pentecost. The Holy Spirit is present within His church. He lives within every believer. The thing that needs to happen is for us to yield to the Holy Spirit. As we become available to Him for witness, His power begins to be manifested.

At conversion the Holy Spirit initiates five transactions

within the believer. The believer is born of the Spirit, baptized of the Spirit, indwelt by the Spirit, sealed by the Spirit, and filled with the Spirit.

Born of the Spirit

First, the believer is born of the Spirit of God (John 3:3-5). The believer does not receive Jesus at one time, then, subsequently, receive the Holy Spirit. "If any man have not the Spirit of Christ, he is none of his" (Rom. 8:9). No one can be saved apart from the life-giving power of the Holy Spirit.

Baptized of the Spirit

Second, every saved person is baptized by the Holy Spirit at conversion. "For by one Spirit are we all baptized into one body, whether we be Jews or Gentiles, whether we be bond or free; and have been made to drink into one Spirit" (1 Cor. 12:13). Through spiritual baptism believers are incorporated into the body of Christ by the Holy Spirit. They are brought into union with Jesus and into unity with other believers.

Indwelt by the Spirit

Third, every believer is indwelt by the Holy Spirit. "What? know ye not that your body is the temple of the Holy Ghost which is in you, which ye have of God, and ye are not your own? For ye are bought with a price: therefore glorify God in your body, and in your spirit, which are God's" (1 Cor. 6:19-20). The Holy Spirit lives in every believer to bring glory to God. We are His possessions. He works through the life of His child.

Sealed by the Spirit

Fourth, every believer is sealed by the Holy Spirit. "In whom also after that ye believed, ye were sealed with that holy Spirit of promise, Which is the earnest of our inheritance until the redemption of the purchased possession, unto the praise of his glory" (Eph. 1:13-14). "Grieve not the holy Spirit of God, whereby ye are sealed unto the day of redemption" (Eph. 4:30).

The Holy Spirit is God's seal or stamp within the life of the believer. The word for *seal* was used in New Testament times in several ways.

A king used his signet ring to make an impression in wax on a document to designate it as official. The Holy Spirit is God's designation that we have come into His family. We have received a Spirit of adoption (see Rom. 8:15).

The word *seal* was used as a guarantee. The Holy Spirit is God's guarantee to us that He will complete our redemption. When we place a postage stamp on a letter, our government guarantees that the letter will get to the person to whom it is sent. God places the Holy Spirit in our lives as His guarantee that He will get us to the point where He promised. He will finish what He began.

Filled with the Spirit

Fifth, every believer is filled with the Holy Spirit at conversion. When sin is confessed, Christ is received; the Holy Spirit comes in to take full control. "Be not drunk with wine, wherein is excess; but be filled with the Holy Spirit" (Eph. 5:18).

The first four transactions of the Holy Spirit are made once for all. They are nonrecurring. There is one spiritual birth, one baptism of the Spirit, one indwelling and sealing of the Spirit. But there are many fillings. We are filled with the Holy Spirit at conversion, but the fullness may not be maintained. When an act of disobedience is committed, one is no longer filled with (under the control of) the Holy Spirit.[5]

Ephesians 5:18 indicates that being filled with the Holy Spirit is a continuing process. One translation has it: "Keep on being filled with the Holy Spirit."[6]

For the fullness of the Spirit to be restored, there must be repentance, confession of sin, and obedience to Him. "Confess and be filled" is the call to victorious living. When sin is confessed, the life is yielded and abandoned to Jesus. He takes control to guide and empower.

Confidence for bold witnessing comes through the ministry of the Holy Spirit. Christians can have abiding confidence that anytime they share Christ with another person it will be successful. It will be successful because of the principles of ministry of the Spirit.

God uses three things in the work of the Holy Spirit to bring people to Himself. God uses the activity of the Holy Spirit through the Word of God. He uses the ministry of the Holy Spirit through the witness of the believer. Then, God uses the direct work of the Holy Spirit in the life of the nonbeliever for conversion.

First, the Bible, the Word of the living God, is used as the instrument of the Holy Spirit to bring people to Christ.[7] "Take the helmet of salvation, and the sword of the Spirit, which is the word of God" (Eph. 6:17).

The Word of God is the sword of the Holy Spirit to penetrate and open the heart to the Spirit for His work. It gives the Holy Spirit admission into the human heart to do His work of conviction.

> For the Word of God is quick, and powerful, and sharper than any two-edged sword, piercing even to the dividing asunder of soul and spirit, and of the joints and marrow, and is a discerner of the thoughts and intents of the heart (Heb. 4:12).

The Word of God is alive and active. It is powerful. Like a two-edged sword, it penetrates. It separates. It divides the issues. It discerns or judges the thoughts and attitudes behind the thoughts.

People who come to church sometimes feel that the preacher has been "reading their mail." They come out of church saying, "Preacher, you might as well have called my name." The preacher might not have even known they were present. He preached the Word. The Word of God discerns the thoughts and intents of the heart.

Human counsel is good if it is right. It can help in many situations. But human counsel cannot penetrate the deepest recesses of a person's being. It cannot meet the deepest needs of one's life. The soul of a person includes the mind, emotion, and will. Human counsel can be an aid in the area of a person's mind. It can assist with a person's thinking. Human counsel can be helpful in the area of emotion. Effective human counsel can guide a person's feelings. In the area of the will, human guidance can be given. Counsel is certainly helpful in making decisions. But human counsel cannot reach into the deep spirit level of a person.

Only the dynamic, powerful Word of God can probe deeply into the spirit level. When it does, it confronts, convicts, enlightens, guides, and comforts. The Word of God builds faith. "So then faith cometh by hearing, and hearing by the word of God" (Rom. 10:17). Faith is not built by an examination of all religions of the world or by analyzing all philosophical systems. Faith is built through hearing the revealed Word of God.

The Word of God is "precious" seed to be sown. When it is sown, God guarantees a harvest. Once the seed is sown, the Holy Spirit waters and cultivates. "He that goeth forth and weepeth, bearing precious seed, shall doubtless come again with rejoicing, bringing his sheaves with him" (Ps. 126:6).

The Holy Spirit directs the Word of God so that it accomplishes what God intends.

> So shall my word be that goeth forth out of my mouth: it shall not return unto me void, but it shall accomplish that which I please, and it shall prosper in the thing whereto I sent it (Isa. 55:11).

Power for effective witness is available by the work of the Spirit through His ministry of the Word.

Second, the Holy Spirit works through the witness of the believer to bring people to Jesus.[8] God uses people to reach people. People are not reached in a vacuum apart from the witness of God's people. I have never met a person anywhere who was saved without any contact with a believer. The Holy Spirit moves through the personality of a Christian to reach out and touch those who need Christ.

Of all the people I have known and testimonies I have heard, the one who came closest to conversion without contact with a believer was a pastor's wife named Masa. She grew up on an isolated island in the Philippines. When she was a little girl, a group of Jehovah Witnesses came through and left a copy of their Bible with her family. The family did not read it. But Masa did. She was interested. But she did not accept Christ and commit her life openly to Him until she came to San Francisco at about twenty-one years of age. It was then that she met believers who shared Christ with her. Immediately, she responded and committed her life. The lost are saved as believers share the Word of God, and the Holy Spirit does His work.

Believers cannot save people. But anywhere there are churches filled with dynamic witnessing believers sharing Christ with others, people are being saved. There will be a climate of spiritual revival.

Wherever churches and believers ignore Jesus' command to witness, those churches die. Few people will be saved in that kind of situation.

People are saved as a witness shares God's Word with them. Witnesses plant and water; God gives the increase. "I have planted, Apollos watered; but God gave the increase" (1 Cor. 3:6).

A tremendous biblical illustration of the fact that God reaches people through His people is Cornelius in Acts 10:5-6. Cornelius was a God fearer. He was seeking God. God sent an angel to him. The angel told him not how to be saved but where to find out how to be saved. The angel told him to send for Simon Peter who would tell him how to be saved. God did not choose to use an angel as a bearer of His redemptive message. Angels have never experienced grace. God has chosen to send people saved by grace as His messengers of redemption. As Peter's Spirit-filled life touched the life of Cornelius, Peter spoke the Word to him and Cornelius was saved.

Another illustration is Acts 8:29-30. The eunuch was reading the Word. But he was not saved. He had a seeking heart. Philip was preaching in a great revival in Samaria. The Holy Spirit told Philip to go to the desert of Gaza. Philip was obedient. His path crossed the path of the Ethiopian eunuch. The man was reading from the Scriptures. What a coincidence! No! This was not a coincidence. It was a God-incidence!

Philip asked him, "Do you understand what you are reading?" (v. 30, NIV).

The answer came, "How can I, except some man should guide me?" (v. 31).

Philip began there, and shared Jesus wwith him. Philip gently took the hand of this searching lost man and guided him through the conversion experience.

God uses human instrumentality to bear the good news of Jesus to people that they might be born of the Spirit. When believers are faithful to the commission to share Jesus in the power of the Holy Spirit, no barrier will stop the onward progress of the gospel. Multitudes will be saved.

Third, God uses the work of the Holy Spirit in the life of nonbelievers to bring them to Christ. Through the witness of a believer, the Word of God, the sword of the Spirit is shared with the nonbeliever. Using the Word, the Holy Spirit penetrates the heart, mind, and soul of the nonbeliever. The lost are spiritually blind. The natural person cannot understand the things of the Spirit of God. He is in darkness. He is like the person who attempts to walk through a totally dark room. He stumbles his way through life. He must have the enlightenment of the Spirit of God in his mind.

> But if our gospel be hid, it is hid to them that are lost: In whom the god of this world hath blinded the minds of them which believe not, lest the light of the glorious gospel of Christ, who is the image of God, should shine unto them (2 Cor. 4:3-4).

Jerry was spiritually blind. He had been exposed to the gospel, but as a natural man he could not understand the things that are of God. His wife witnessed to him; numbers of her church member friends and leaders witnessed to him. It made no impression.

One Easter he attended church and heard the simple story of the steps of Jesus to the cross. The following Wednesday night I had the unmistakable impression that I must visit Jerry after prayer meeting. A deacon and I knocked on his door. He gladly welcomed us.

He said, "Preacher, I am glad you came. Ever since Sunday I have been thinking about Jesus and the cross." I listened as he continued to tell me what he understood of Jesus' death and what it meant to him. It was as though a light had come on. His darkness was gone. The Holy Spirit had done His work of enlightenment.

When I asked if we could pray and if he would receive Christ, he shouted to his wife, "Come in here! We are going to pray with the preacher." Soon, he was saved. The Holy Spirit does the work of enlightenment so that persons can come to Christ.

The lost are separated from God. Christ has bridged the gap of separation between God and persons. But it is the Holy Spirit who draws people to God through Christ. Jesus said, "No man can come to me, except the Father which hath sent me draw him" (John 6:44).

The lost are all under sin (see Rom. 3:9). God is holy. Persons are sinful. A sin barrier exists between humanity and

God. It separates a person from God. He comes under sin's dominion and power. Sin occupies the position of authority over his life.

The lost are in sin. "I said therefore unto you, that ye shall die in your sins: for if ye believe not that I am he, ye shall die in your sins" (John 8:24).

Deliverance comes through the power of the Holy Spirit.

> He will reprove the world of sin, and of righteousness, and of judgment: Of sin, because they believe not on me; Of righteousness, because I go to my Father, and ye see me no more; Of judgment, because the prince of the world is judged (John 16:8-11).

The Holy Spirit shows nonbelievers where they are wrong. The Holy Spirit convicts of sin. He reveals to lost persons the realm of their living. He reveals the fact that the lost are separated from God by their sins. The lost begin to realize that they are under bondage. The Holy Spirit reveals that unbelief is what keeps them separated from God.

The Holy Spirit convicts of righteousness. Jesus is God's standard of righteousness. He has gone to the Father; the world sees Him no more. The Holy Spirit reveals the righteousness of Jesus to the heart and mind of a lost person. As a lost person sees his own sinful life in comparison to the righteousness of Jesus, he is convicted. If he responds to the Holy Spirit, his heart will be humbled to brokenness and repentance.

The Holy Spirit convicts of judgment. Judgment is sure. The prince of this world (Satan) has been judged and sentenced. Every person outside of Christ is judged already. The Holy Spirit reveals the terror of judgment to the mind and heart of a lost one. He reveals Christ as the only way of deliverance.[9]

The lost are enemies of God (Rom. 5:10). They are at war with God. "But the wicked are like the troubled sea, when it cannot rest, whose waters cast up mire and dirt. There is no peace, saith my God, to the wicked" (Isa. 57:20-21). Like the constant churning of the waves of the sea, the heart of the lost person is perpetually restless. There is incessant turmoil and unrest in a lost person's life. Like the sea, the waters of lost lives pour forth filth and depravity. The lost are spiritually dead. "The wages of sin is death" (Rom. 6:23). The Holy Spirit brings the lost person to a point of surrender. The war is over. Like Paul, he will cry out, "Lord, what wilt thou have me to do?" (Acts 9:6).

Paul declared to the Ephesian Christians that they were dead in trespasses and sins. Lost humanity must be made alive. The Holy Spirit regenerates dead spiritual lives. "Jesus answered, Verily, verily, I say unto thee, Except a man be born of water and of the Spirit, he cannot enter into the kingdom of God" (John 3:5). It is the Spirit that makes alive.

The complementary work of three is adequate to bring the lost to Jesus Christ. God uses the Word of God, the witness of the believer, and the work of the Holy Spirit to bring people to Christ.

Adequate Power Is Available

To implement Jesus' strategy of reaching our world, He has provided adequate power through the Holy Spirit. Let the church be the church. Let local churches all over this world get back to the strategy of Jesus. Make the program of the church witness unto Jesus. Adopt His plan for penetration of our communities until the gospel is extended to the ends of the earth. Equip every believer to share Christ in the power of the Holy Spirit.

When the church in faithfulness steps out under the marching orders of its Lord, it will penetrate this earth with the gospel of Jesus Christ. No barriers will stop the onward movement of the gospel. The circle of witness power will continue to extend until it encompasses the globe. *The gates of hell cannot prevail against it!*

Questions

1. In what ways could you improve the evangelizing activity of the laity in your church?

2. What recent demonstration of the Holy Spirit's power have you observed in your church?

10 Envision the Strategy:

Planning an Evangelistic Church Growth Strategy

Our country can be reached with the gospel. The team and the strategy are in place. Local churches in every community in the United States are capable of reaching their areas with the gospel. Within these churches is a mighty army for God, an army of laypeople ready to follow their pastor and leaders in taking their communities for Christ. Pastors inspire the laity for evangelism through their own model of personal witnessing. Pastors are the key to enlightening the laity regarding the mission of reaching people, enlisting and equipping the laity for the task of intentional witnessing, engaging and encouraging the laity in the church's program of evangelism, and for life-style, intentional witnessing. Together pastor and people can impact a community for Christ.

The resources are available to reach our country for Christ. They have been given by a sovereign Lord for such a time as this. People everywhere are open to the gospel. God has provided the message, the manpower, and the money for reaching them for Christ. The challenge of every church is to maximize their use of both in reaching the lost for Christ.

Reaching its area means the church will not be satisfied with growing by transferring members from other churches or just by baptizing family members. A church that reaches its community and grows will need an evangelistic church growth strategy.

Evangelistic Church Growth Strategy Essentials

Total Church Life is a resource for a local church in developing an evangelistic church growth strategy. Like any strategy it requires study and application. This chapter provides specific application of the principles presented in the first nine chapters of this book. These principles are applicable to a church of any size and cultural background. They require adaptation for each individual church setting.

A Spirit of Reviving Power

The first essential is a spirit of reviving power. Revival is a must for dynamic and effective evangelism. Dead churches do not grow. Like the church of Ephesus in Revelation 2:4, the "first love" of every church tends to cool. Evangelism wanes. Leonard Sanderson quoted C. E. Matthews, who said, "It is our tendency to move away *from* rather than *toward* evangelism." Every church is moving toward plateau and eventual decline unless revival is experienced. Two factors are involved:

Divine Intervention

God's activity through His Spirit must move to cleanse the church from three things: self-interests, clinging to its comfort zones, and lack of love for Christ. Worked-up enthusiasm and organizational effort cannot revive the church and cause it to grow. A revived church is motivated and energized by the Spirit for the mission of Christ. A spiritual awakening sweeping across our land to bring revival to the churches is essential to reach America for Christ.

As noted in chapter 9, the Holy Spirit provides power for witness and for reviving a church. Reviving power is available to all Christians. It comes through prayer that prevails and preaching and teaching about the Holy Spirit, sin, repentance, and obedience. An evangelism strategy is powerless without the control and involvement of the Holy Spirit.

Diagnostic Initiative

A diagnosis of the church's current status is a second factor in reviving the church and getting it growing again. Healing always begins with a diagnosis of the problem. An effective strategy can be implemented when a church determines why they are growing slowly or why they are not growing at all. The following are two diagnostic tools to determine the church's current health.

First is the diagnostic tool of *position* assessment, which determines the present stage of the church's life. Every church moves through various stages of development.

Churches tend to plateau and decline after they have grown to strength and affluence. The nation is full of formerly growing churches—churches that became like the church in Ephesus. The Ephesus Tendency describes the tendency for organizations and churches to lose their vitality.

The church of Ephesus, a missionary church planted by Paul in the first century, went through several stages. They include:

Struggle, as the church is planted and begins its ministry.

Surrender, as it depends upon the Lord and obeys Him in its life and mission.

Success, as it becomes fruitful and grows.

Satisfaction, as it enjoys the blessing of growth and vitality.

Self-centeredness, as it turns its attention inward rather than keeping its mission primary.

A continued atmosphere of self-interest results in plateau; then, stagnation, stress, decline, dissension, deterioration, defeat, and deadness. Every church faces the reality of

Diagram 10.1

ENVISION THE STRATEGY

EPHESUS TENDENCY
Diagnosing Current Status

**PLATEAU
STAGNATION – STRESS**

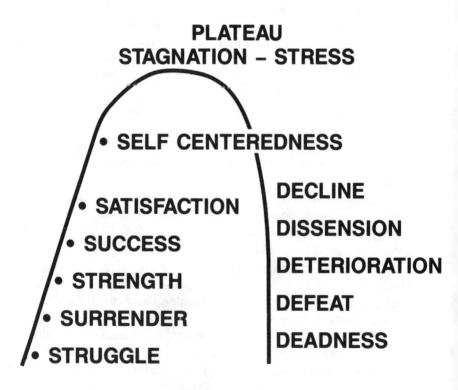

- **SELF CENTEREDNESS**

- **SATISFACTION**
- **SUCCESS**
- **STRENGTH**
- **SURRENDER**
- **STRUGGLE**

DECLINE

DISSENSION

DETERIORATION

DEFEAT

DEADNESS

the Ephesus Tendency. Study diagram 10.1 to diagnose what stage the church is in.

The church in Ephesus began with Paul ministering in the marketplace and winning converts. He taught and equipped them to win others. For two years he apparently did not leave the city, yet Acts 19:10 states that within that period "all they which dwelt in Asia heard the word of the Lord Jesus." It happened through the witness of those who were saved and went everywhere evangelizing.

Ephesus was alive! The church participated in implementing Jesus' commission in Acts 1:8. They saturated their geographic area with the gospel. They shared Christ with every person.

However, by the end of the century, the Lord instructed John to tell the church of Ephesus that they had left their first love. He warned them to repent and do again the first work or else He would remove their candlestick from its place. The church had left its first work of getting the gospel to every person because it had left its fervent love for Jesus. Indeed, the tendency is to move away from rather than toward evangelism.

The great question is "Can vitality be restored?" Jesus' counsel indicates that the Ephesus Tendency can be overcome. "Remember the height from which you have fallen! Repent and do the things you did at first" (Rev. 2:5, NIV).

"Remember" would involve the church in diagnosing its current status. "Repent" means more than an emotional response of sorrow and regret for the church's condition. It involves change in the church. The church that reinforces its current status and resists change continues in plateau and eventual decline. Change is inevitable. It will happen! The attitude of "we like our church like it is and want to keep it that way" brings negative change. The church must have the flexibility to adjust and respond positively to what God is doing if it is to grow again. It must "do the things it did at first" on mission for Christ, the Head of the church. A church can rebound from the Ephesus Tendency of stagnation and decline. The three components of the Total Church Life strategy are effective to enable churches to grow again.

The second diagnostic tool is a *priority* assessment. It helps the church examine its priorities and implement the changes that will effect growth. If God gave revival today, many churches would stifle it in two weeks by refusing to make necessary changes. Three priority decisions determine whether or not any church will grow. They are:

1. A time decision—calendar
2. A money decision—budgeting/assigning
3. A people decision—electing/assigning

Priority Decision One: A Time Decision—Calendar. If people are to be reached, evangelism must be scheduled into the calendar. Prime time must be given for the priority work of enlisting and equipping laity, prospect discovery, witness and soul-winning visitation, evangelistic saturation, evangelistic crusades, revival meetings, and other special events. If evangelism is not planned and entered into the calendar as a priority in our personal and church schedules, not much will be done. We will fill our weeks, days, and hours with other things, perhaps good things but secondary things.

For consistent evangelistic outreach, a church should set aside one day per week for evangelistic visitation. Evangelistic outreach will be discussed later in the chapter.

The time decision includes completing an evangelistic planning calendar like can be found on pages 209-210. It is discussed later in the chapter. Make the time commitment to develop an evangelism calendar for the church.

A word of caution is needed at this point. Evangelism as a priority must not be delegated away from the pastor. The evangelistic leadership of the pastor is essential and urgent for the church to be permeated with an evangelistic spirit. It has been said that if people bleed for souls, the pastor must hemorrhage. The church should secure the most qualified and capable laypersons to serve on the church evangelism council. An excellent resource to guide in the organization and work of the council is *The Church Evangelism Manual*. It is available through the Home Mission Board.

Every church and organizational leader should be equipped for intentional witnessing. They should be led to understand and participate in the church's goal to enlist and equip every member for intentional witnessing. Specific suggestions are provided in the discussion of the evangelism calendar. God is providing all that is needed to reach the United States for Christ. Set the priority of evangelism in the church's time, money, and people decisions.

Priority Decision Two: A Money Decision—Budgeting. If people are to be reached for Christ, money must be budgeted annually to implement the strategy of total evangelism. Programs to enlist and equip the laity cost money. Materials and methods for saturating an area with the gospel cost money. Revivals, evangelistic equipping, evangelistic campaigns, and events will cost money if they are to be effective today. Priority money must be budgeted for evangelism if the "first work" gets done. The church should budget at least a tithe, 10 percent, to evangelism events and activities.

Priority Decision Three: A People Decision—Electing and Assigning. If people are to be reached for Christ, effective leaders must be sought and elected to lead in prioritizing evangelism. A church will do well to structure in its organization a church evangelism council to assist the pastor with the church's strategy, planning, and programming for evangelism. Some churches may choose to function with an evangelism director rather than a council. The council will be discussed more completely later in the chapter.

Diagnosing the church's present position is a good start to developing an effective evangelistic church growth strategy. Once that is determined the church can implement the second and third essentials to an evangelistic church growth strategy.

A Strategy for Reaching People

The second essential for planning an evangelistic church growth strategy includes a comprehensive plan for growth in every area of the church. The organization and structure of the church must grow to assimilate the new converts. Review chapter 4 on organization and administration for church growth.

Three Components of a Strategy

The outline for this book provides three components that have proven effective for church growth. Use this outline to evaluate the church-growth strategy. Be sure to evaluate every aspect of the church so new members will be welcomed and involved. Every part of the church should Exalt the Savior, Equip the Saints, and Evangelize the Sinner.

Methodology of Jesus

Planning an evangelistic church growth strategy should begin with a review of the evangelistic method of Jesus described in chapter 8. The strategic method of Jesus given in Acts 1:8 involves: (1) A Program, (2) A Plan, (3) Personnel, (4) A Power.

Evangelism Techniques in the Early Church

Establishing an evangelistic church growth strategy can be powerfully implemented by following the patterns and principles of a balance in evangelistic techniques. Chapter 8 discussed how the early church blended together the following five basic techniques to fulfill the strategy of total evangelism:
1. Public Proclamation
2. Caring Affirmation and Ministry
3. Event Attraction
4. Geographic Saturation
5. Personal Presentation

A church strategy would benefit from incorporating those five elements.

Two Priorities for a Strategy

The strategy of Jesus and the early church had two priorities. Jesus and the early church were involved in TOTAL PENETRATION of the community through TOTAL PARTICIPATION of the members in witness. The evangelistic church growth strategy of any church must include those two priorities as discussed in chapter 8.

A Structure for Renewing Priorities

The third and final essential to planning an evangelistic church growth strategy is developing a structure for renewing priorities. The diagnostic tools of time, money, and people have been discussed. The twofold strategic priorities of Total Penetration and Total Participation have also been presented. So how does a congregation develop a structure that includes those priorities in the church?

There are twelve activities involved in setting a structure that renews priorities.

(1) Lead the Church in a Total Church Life Seminar

Have every leader in the church read the book *Total Church Life*. Then go through the text in a seminar. There are four options for attending a Total Church Life Seminar.

Attend a seminar near the church.—Total Church Life Seminars are being held by many state conventions and associations. The Seminar is also offered each year at the HMB sponsored Schools of Evangelism and Church Growth and at Home Missions weeks in Glorieta and Ridgecrest.

Conduct a seminar in the church with a guest leader.— Guest leaders are available by contacting the state director of evangelism or the Evangelism Section of the Home Mission Board.

Use the Total Church Life Resource Kit to present a seminar in the church.—A *Total Church Life Resource Kit* is available from the Home Mission Board. It provides teaching aids to present Total Church Life in eight fifty-to-eighty-minute sessions. The *Resource Kit* includes a *Leader's Guide,* overhead cells, a *Resource Kit Video* and other materials.

Use the Total Church Life Video Seminar. An eight-session seminar is available from the Home Mission Board on four videotapes. Each session contains a forty-five-minute video presentation by the author. The seminar packet also contains a *Video Teacher's Guide* and a *Video Viewer's Guide* to facilitate discussion and application.

(2) Preach Through Total Church Life

A second activity to change structure is to preach messages on the principles found in *Total Church Life.* The pastor can encourage the people to plan an evangelistic church growth strategy by preaching through the scriptural basis of the book.

(3) Begin or Revitalize an Evangelism Council

Materials are available from the state directors of evangelism and the Home Mission Board on the Church Evangelism Council. Every church needs a council to assist the pastor to emphasize evangelism and missions. The council can help to plan and implement each of the following structure-changing activities. A Church Missions Development Council (CMDC) can also be effective if care is given to keep evangelism a priority. Be sure to have both men and women serving on the Councils.

(4) Define a Geographic Area or Areas

A fourth activity is to define a specific geographic area or areas for which the church will accept responsibility. That responsibility includes saturation with the gospel and sharing Christ with every person. To reach people, a church must have a specific place for total penetration that nurtures people and wins them to Christ. See chapter 8.

(5) Build Prospect Files

The fifth activity is critically important to changing structures for renewing priorities. The evangelistic church growth strategy must have an active and thorough prospect file. The main prospects are every person within the geographic area of the church. Remember though that every person a church member meets is a prospective new Christian. Every one should be witnessed to whether or not they are prospects to attend the church.

Door-to-door canvassing is one of the best ways to discover prospects. The Home Mission Board has a good prospect discovery kit called the *Religious Opinion Survey Packet.* Many public utilities will sell or provide newcomer lists. Mortgage companies and real-estate offices can also be helpful contacts to locate prospects for the church. A bus ministry locates dozens of prospects in the community. Do not neglect multihousing communities in the church field. Evangelistic events also bring prospects to the church. The best prospects, however, come from the church members' circle of influence and acquaintances. Every church member should list family members, neighbors, friends, coworkers, and other contacts as prospects of the church. A new Christian's circle of influence usually can provide many individual prospects and pockets of prospects.

Publicity through local papers, direct mail, billboards, and church signs draws visitors to the church. Train the ushers to identify visitors and be sure the visitors receive a warm welcome and fill out a visitor's card. Follow-up is helpful to be sure the card is filled out and returned. Make it easy for visitors to find where they are to go for Bible Study and worship. Review chapter 8 for more information on discovering and cultivating prospects.

(6) Begin or Revitalize Weekly Evangelistic Outreach

Every church should have weekly evangelistic outreach. The form and structure of the outreach should reflect the cultural background and work schedules of the church members. Contact should include a handwritten letter from a church member, a phone call, and a visit. Include information about the church and a gospel tract in the letters. Visitation teams may need to call first depending on the individual situation and the leadership of the Holy Spirit. Be sure that each in-home visit follows the prompting of the Holy Spirit to include an invitation to know Jesus personally as well as an invitation to church. When people are not at home, leave a brief handwritten note and materials that share Christ and inform about the church.

Evangelistic outreach should be organized through the Sunday School. It should be promoted through all church organizations and by the pastor from the pulpit. The one-night-per-week visitation program is widely used. A visitor to the church should receive an initial follow-up contact the day of the visit. Provide opportunities on visitation night for people to write letters, make phone calls, to go on visitation teams, or provide prayer support. Many churches also have daytime visitation involving retired persons, shift workers, and others who cannot visit at night.

Based on a recent report, 36.8 percent of SBC churches conduct weekly evangelistic visits. It has been stated that 68 percent of all SBC churches are plateaued in their growth or are declining. The two statistics are closely related. Evangelistic visitation is an essential ingredient for reaching people and for church growth. One of the chief characteristics of higher baptism churches is that they conduct an organized weekly evangelistic visitation program.

(7) Set a Baptism Goal

The seventh activity challenges the church to increase both the number and ratio of baptisms. Set a goal to begin baptizing one person for every thirty members. Then increase the goal to one baptism for every twenty members. Many ethnic churches baptize one person for every thirteen members. A good goal eventually is to baptize one person for every ten members. Many smaller-membership churches have a much better baptism ratio than large-membership churches. The ratio of people baptized to number of members is more important than who has the highest number of baptisms in the state. It is important that rebaptisms be counted separately from new convert baptisms.

(8) Have Every Program Set Evangelism as a Priority

The eighth activity challenges every church program to set evangelism as a priority. Have the leaders of each program determine to be personally evangelistic. Then discover ways to provide some sort of evangelistic outreach. Every church program should be responsible for identifying prospects, sharing the gospel, and bringing the lost into a relationship with Jesus Christ.

(9) Have Every Committee Set Evangelism as a Priority

Every church committee can be evangelistic if they choose. Individual committee members should be personally involved in witnessing and soul-winning. The kitchen committee could struggle to be evangelistic. However, they could share Wednesday night supper with a local fire station or needy people. Every week a kitchen committee member could take food to the fire station. As different committee members make friends among the fire fighters, perhaps a Bible Study could begin there.

(10) Begin or Revitalize Training for New Members

New members, particularly new converts, need to learn what it means to be a Christian. Every church needs some kind of new member orientation. Training classes can vary in length from one week to six weeks. At least four topics need to be included:

(1) Review the plan of salvation. Many people have joined a church without having a relationship with Jesus Christ.

(2) Study what Southern Baptists believe and how we operate. A good resource is the *Baptist Faith and Message* from the Sunday School Board. Also review how Baptists differ from other denominations.

(3) Communicate the Total Church Life Strategy to new members. Help them to participate in the evangelistic church growth strategy.

(4) Introduce the layout of the church building and the organization of the church programs and ministries.

Other information can be gained by reviewing "Incorporating New Members" in chapter 7.

(11) Schedule a Leadership Retreat

The eleventh activity for restructuring priorities is to hold a yearly leadership retreat. Held late in the year, the retreat serves to evaluate the year's goals and to set goals for the third year distant. That way the church is always functioning under a three-year evangelistic church growth strategy. Some churches prefer to function with a five-year calendar. The calendar form is easily adaptable to any number of years.

The agenda for the retreat should include spiritual motivation, a study of some facet of evangelistic church growth, and a review of the previous year's church work. The pastor should already personally have thought through needs, opportunities, goals, and plans for the coming year. He should lead the group in brainstorming for planning and goal setting.

Retreats can be held in a variety of settings. It is usually most effective to limit the retreat to one day or a Friday night and Saturday in a casual, convenient setting. Involve the Church Council, deacons, and Sunday School department directors. Make it a fun, relaxed setting but cover the evangelism strategy planning and evaluation.

(12) Create an Evangelism Planning Calendar

Participation in the twelfth activity will revolutionize how the church plans an evangelistic church growth strategy. The following page presents a blank evangelism planning calendar (diagram 10.2).The calendar provides a structure to plan, implement, and prioritize evangelism for church growth. The second page following provides a sample evangelism calendar (diagram 10.3). The calendar, designed by Dr. C. Thomas Wright of the Home Mission Board evangelism section, develops a three-year evangelistic church growth strategy. It includes columns for planning monthly evangelism activities, monthly evangelism equipping events, specific target groups, and yearly evangelistic church growth goals.

Determine the Dates Covered.—Begin by putting at the top of the page the dates for the next three years. As the first year ends, plan the calendar for the third year distant.

Evangelism Equipping Activities.—Fill in any equipping activities usually conducted by the church. Review chapter 7, "Equipping Ministry," for equipping activities. Adapt the activities to the distinctive setting and needs of the church. These activities are intended to teach church members how to be more effective personal witnesses. That includes understanding about other faiths and being able to respond biblically to false teachings.

SAMPLE
Total Church Life Evangelism Strategy Planning Calendar
1996 Through 1998

Church Name: _____

Year 1996	Equipping Activity	Evangelistic Event	Target Group	Year 1997	Equipping Activity	Evangelistic Event	Target Group	Year 1998	Equipping Activity	Evangelistic Event	Target Group
JAN	IFW-New Age		Youth/Adults	JAN				JAN	TCL	Drama in Worship	Senior Adults
FEB	TCL		Church Leaders	FEB	CWT		Church Members	FEB	CWT	Valentine Banquet	Senior & Young Adults
MAR		Spring Revival	Church Members	MAR		Spring Ski Trip	Youth	MAR	Cross-cultural Evangelism	Revival Youth Focus	Youth
APR	One Day Seminar		Sunday School Leaders	APR	TCL	Drama in Worship	All Leaders	APR	IFW-Jehovah's Witnesses	Senior Adult Trip	Senior Adults
MAY		VBS	Children	MAY	WIN School		Sunday Schoo Teach	MAY	One Day S...	Concerts	Church Members
JUNE				JUNE		VBS	Childr Prospe	JUNE	P...S...	VBS-USA	Children
JULY	BWR			JULY	R	Spo... Banquet	Youn Adult Singles	JULY	B...	VBS-Mexico	Youth
AUG		Fall Revival	Members/Ethnics	AUG				AUG	WIN School	Pool Party	Singles
SEPT		Movie	Youth	SEPT	One Day		Senior Adults	SEPT	Cross-cultural Evangelism	ESL Class	Ethnics
OCT	CWT	Clothing Closet/Food Bank	Non-members	OCT	IFW-Mormons	Harvest Festival	Children	OCT	Children's Sunday	Harvest	Children/Prospects
NOV	Stewardship	Month		NOV	Stewardship	Month		NOV	Stewardship	Month	Church Members
DEC		Concert	Members	DEC	Sharing Jesus in Marketplace	Concert	Lay Leaders/Members	DEC	IFW-Buddhism	Concert	Prospects

Year's Evangelistic Church Growth Goals (1996)
1. Baptize one person per 30 members (5)
2. Have one evangelism activity each quarter
3. Have one event each quarter

Year's Evangelistic Church Growth Goals (1997)
1. Baptize one person per 25 members (6)
2. Have two activities per quarter
3. Have two events per quarter

Year's Evangelistic Church Growth Goals (1998)
1. Baptize one person per 20 members (8)
2. Have activities 11 months
3. Have events 11 months

Calendar five years of evangelism strategy. Then as each year ends develop the fifth year's strategy.

Total Church Life Evangelism Strategy Planning Calendar

199___ Through 199___

Church Name _____

Year 199___	Equipping Activity	Evangelistic Event	Target Group	Year 199___	Equipping Activity	Evangelistic Event	Target Group	Year 199___	Equipping Activity	Evangelistic Event	Target Group
JAN				JAN				JAN			
FEB				FEB				FEB			
MAR				MAR				MAR			
APR				APR				APR			
MAY				MAY				MAY			
JUNE				JUNE				JUNE			
JULY				JULY				JULY			
AUG				AUG				AUG			
SEPT				SEPT				SEPT			
OCT				OCT				OCT			
NOV				NOV				NOV			
DEC				DEC				DEC			
Year's Evangelistic Church Growth Goals				Year's Evangelistic Church Growth Goals				Year's Evangelistic Church Growth Goals			

Calendar five years of evangelism strategy. Then as each year ends develop the fifth year's strategy.

Revival meetings, harvest crusades, music events, age and interest group events, Lay Renewal Weekends, Lay Discipleship Weekends, Prayer for Spiritual Awakening Conferences, Interfaith Witness training seminars and classes, ministry evangelism activities, and other such events should be scheduled to grow the spiritual life of a church and to reach the lost for Christ. Each January, Soul-Winning Commitment Day should be observed. Prospect discovery programs such as door-to-door witness and survey, People Search, telephone surveys, Sunday School enrollment campaigns, and Bible literature distribution should be conducted periodically to saturate an area and to discover prospects.

Of course, no church can do all of these programs in a given year. But continue to implement the priorities of totally penetrating the church's geographic area with a gospel witness through total participation of the church's membership. The approach will enhance a church's organized program of evangelism and will result in inspiring and equipping believers for intentional life-style witnessing. It will involve church members in the everyday process of marketplace evangelism.

Evangelistic Events.—Fill in all of the evangelistic activities usually done by the church. Most churches have Vacation Bible School and a fall or spring revival or both. Review the discussion on evangelistic events in chapter 8. Begin the first year with a goal to have at least one event every quarter. Gradually increase the initial goal to at least one event every month. Be sure to provide specific events for every target group in the community. Adapt events to the needs of the community and be creative to develop new events.

The design of a church's long-range evangelism calendar would do well to incorporate the *WIN School: A Lay Evangelism Strategy* as the basic equipping program. It will set the soul-winning direction of the church by involving the total church membership. A WIN School is designed to disciple believers in living the Christian life and to train them in the basic techniques of leading the lost to Christ. *Continuing Witness Training (CWT)* should be an ongoing program of intensive witness training of individual church members. CWT is led by equippers in a one-on-one approach.

Interspersed between *WIN Schools*, additional equipping programs should be used for further training and motivation. Some of these are: *Lifestyle Witnessing for Women* and *Building Witnessing Relationships (BWR)* to equip in relational Evangelism. The *One Day Soul-Winning Workshop,* Marked New Testament, and *People Sharing Jesus* are also effective.

The leadership should be formally equipped through participating in any effective intentional witness program the church may designate. Every staff person, deacon, music leader, missions leader, training leader, Bible study leader, outreach leader, and committee chairperson should be included.

Determine Target Group.—The target group is the segment of the church or community that is to be reached by that event or activity. Target groups include specific ethnic groups, senior adults, "yuppies," young marrieds, single again, singles, youth, and children. Other target groups include language groups, specific housing areas, and specific vocations. The church should welcome all people. However, they should also realize that people prefer to come to Jesus by crossing the least number of social, cultural, and linguistic barriers.

Set Yearly Evangelism Goals.—The next page provides space to write down the yearly evangelism goals. Include the baptism goal and outreach goals, increasing the number and types of events and activities, and varying target groups. Update the calendar every year at the leadership retreat or another prearranged time.

Questions

1. Respond to the Ephesus Tendency.

On a scale of 1 to 10 with 1 being plateaued and 10 being alive and growing, where would you rate your church?

2. What kind of structure does your church have for a yearly evaluation of evangelistic priorities?

3. What does your church calendar say about your church's priorities?

4. What does the term "intentional witnessing" mean to you?

5. If total evangelism results in the planting of new churches, where could your church begin a mission, chapel, or fellowship?

Conclusion

The implementation of the strategy is now in your hands. Here are several questions that will help you deveop your own Total Church Life evangelistic church growth strategy. A discussion of these questions is found in the *Total Church Life Leader's Guide* in the Total Church Life Resource Kit available from the Home Mission Board.

What motivational methods can be used to encourage evangelistic growth in your church? In what ways could you make evangelistic church growth a part of everything your church does? What methods of equipping would be best suited to your church?

How can the laity become involved in personal evangelistic church growth? How can the laity become *more* involved in personal evangelistic church growth? What methods can be used for the continuing encouragement of lay involvement?

What types of mass evangelism events would be best suited for your church and community? What would be the best time and place for these events?

What groups of people live within outreach of your

church? What special activities—such as revival meetings, music events, drama presentations and telemarketing—could be planned to reach individuals in these groups?

What follow-up materials for new believers could be best used by your church? How long will the follow-up last? At what point will you teach the new believer to witness?

What kind of prayer support can be established for evangelistic church growth? How much priority will be placed on prayer?

Total Church Life can be a seminar or a strategy. It can be effective for a few hours or for the life of the church. As a strategy it requires at least two years to implement. It is not a quick-fix to church growth. Total Church Life addresses the underlying priorities of the church.

Total evangelism will inevitably result in planting new churches in every pocket of population in the United States. They will be centers for evangelism and ministry as the cycle of winning people to Christ, equipping them, and starting additional churches continues. Every local church and mission can be a dynamic, Bible-believing, witnessing, ministering body of Christ reaching people for Christ and planting churches in every community in America.

The team is in place to reach America for Christ. Let that mighty army of God in our churches rise up and move forward on their mission to take this country for Christ.

Notes

Introduction

1. Arthur Percy Fitt, *The Life of D. L. Moody* (Chicago: Moody Press n.d.,), 39.

2. W. E. Vine, *Expository Dictionary of New Testament Words* (McLean, Va.: MacDonald Publishing Company, n.d.,), 85-86.

3. Edward T. Hiscox, *The New Directory for Baptist Churches* (Philadelphia: Judson Press, 1956), 22*ff.*

4. Herschel H. Hobbs, *Fundamentals of our Faith* (Nashville: Tenn.: Broadman Press, 1960), 127-29.

5. Ibid.

6. J. Clyde Turner, *The New Testament Doctrine of the Church* (Nashville: Convention Press, 1951), 35.

7. Ibid., 37-38.

8. Elton Trueblood, *The Company of the Committed* (New York, Evanston, and London: Harper and Row, 1962), 68-75.

Chapter 1

1. Raymond W. Hurn, *Finding Your Ministry* (Kansas City, Mo.: Beacon Hill Press, 1979), 35.

2. Ray C. Stedman, *Body Life* (Glendale, Calif.: Regal, 1972), 56-57.

3. Jack W. MacGorman, *The Gifts of the Spirit* (Nashville: Tenn.: Broadman Press, 1974), 46-47.

4. Alan Cole, *The Body of Christ* (Philadelphia, Pa.: Westminster Press, 1964), 45-46.

5. W. A. Criswell, *The Holy Spirit in Today's World* (Grand Rapids: Mich.: Zondervan Publishing House, 1966), 125-32.

Chapter 2

1. Ray C. Stedman, *Body Life* (Glendale, Calif.: Regal, 1972), 31-36.

2. Gerhard Kittel, *Theological Dictionary of the New Testament* (Grand Rapids, Mich.: Eerdmans Publishing Co., 1965), 3:804-8.

3. Ibid., 5:199-215.

4. Keith Miller, *Taste of New Wine* (Waco, Tex.: Word Books, 1965), 58-59.

5. Kittel, 3:413-26.

6. William Barclay, *The Acts of the Apostles* (Philadelphia: The Westminster Press, 1955), 79.

7. E. M. Blaiklock, *The Acts of the Apostles* (Grand Rapids: Eerdmans, 1974), 65-66.

8. Ibid., 68-69.

9. Vine, *Expository Dictionary*, 775.

10. David A. Womack, *The Pyramid Principle of Church Growth* (Minneapolis: Bethany Fellowship, 1977), 16.

Chapter 3

1. Hobbs, *Fundamentals*, 129-31.

2. Jay E. Adams, *Pastoral Leadership* (Grand Rapids: Baker Book House, 1975), 13-14.

3. Edward T. Hiscox, *The New Directory for Baptist Churches*, (Philadelphia: Judson Press, 1956), 100-01.

4. Robert E. Naylor, *The Baptist Deacon* (Nashville: Broadman Press, 1955), 79.

5. Howard B. Foshee, *The Ministry of the Deacon* (Nashville, Tenn.: Convention Press, 1969), 79.

6. Hiscox, *Directory for Baptist Churches*, 160-215.

Chapter 4

1. Paul W. Powell, *The Nuts and Bolts of Church Growth* (Nashville, Tenn.: Broadman Press, 1982), 62-63.

2. Jay Adams, *Christian Counsellor's Manual* (Grand Rapids, Mich.: Baker Book House, 1973), 348-67.

3. Ronald W. Willingham, *Success for You* (Amarillo: Tex.: Goals Unlimited Corp., 1968), chap. 11.

4. Alan Lakein, How to Get Control of Your Time and Your Life (Times Mirror, Signet: New American Library, 1973), pp. 43-68.

5. Edward R. Dayton and Ted W. Engstrom, *Strategy for Living: How to Make the Best Use of Your Time and Abilities* (Ventura, Calif.: Regal Books, 1976), 14-25.

6. Norman Vincent Peale, *Enthusiasm Makes the Difference* (Englewood Cliffs, N.J.: Prentice Hall, 1967), 103.

Chapter 5

1. John W. Humble, *How to Manage by Objectives* (AMACOM, a Division of American Management Associations: 1972), 74-94.

2. Frank T. Hardesty, *Communications* (Columbia, S.C.: Educational Resources Foundation, 1973), 34-40.

3. Ibid., 27-28.

4. Arthur Flake, *Building a Standard Sunday School* (Nashville: Tenn.: Sunday School Board SBC., 1922), 112-13.

Chapter 6

1. Paul Benjamin, *The Equipping Ministry* (Cincinnati, Ohio: Standard Publishing, 1952), 11-18.

2. Kenneth Scott Latourette, *A History of Christianity* (New York: Harper and Brothers Publishers, 1953), 183.

3. Benjamin, 29-34.

Chapter 7

1. Ray C. Stedman, *Body Life* (Glendale, Calif., Regal Books, 1972), 80-82.

2. Kenneth A. Wuest, *Word Studies in the Greek New Testament* (Grand Rapids, Mich.: Eerdmans, 1966). 2:150-51.

3. Leslie B. Flynn, *Nineteen Gifts of the Spirit* (Wheaton, Ill.: Victor Books, 1975), 23-36.

4. Frank B. Minirth, *Christian Psychiatry* (Old Tappan, N.J.: Fleming H. Revell Company, 1977), 37-38.

Chapter 8

1. J. E. Conant, *Every Member Evangelism* (New York and Evanston: Harper & Row, 1992), 91-94.

2. Blaiklock, *Acts*, 30.

3. Leighton Ford, *The Christian Persuader* (New York: Harper & Row Publishers, 1966), 41-53.

4. Barclay, *Acts*, 4.

Chapter 9

1. Lay Evangelism School, WIN Teacher's Manual (Baptist General Convention of Texas, Evangelism Division, n.d.), 5.

2. Gene Edwards, *How to Have a Soul-Winning Church* (Springfield, Mo.: Gospel Publishing House, 1962), 27.

3. Benjamin, *Equipping Ministry*, 68.

4. Robert G. Witty, *Holy Spirit Power* (Jacksonville, Fla.: Pioneer Press, 1966), 59.

5. Ibid., 51-55.

6. W. A. Criswell, *The Holy Spirit*, 109-10.

7. W. A. Criswell, *Why I Preach that the Bible Is Literally True* (Nashville, Tenn.: Broadman Press, 1969), 12-13.

8. James A. Stewart, *The Phenomena of Pentecost* (Alexandria, La.: Lamplighter Publications, 1969), 44-46.

9. A. J. Gordon, *The Ministry of the Spirit* (Philadelphia: American Baptist Publication Society, 1895), 187-89.

Bibliography

Anderson, Leith. *Dying for Change*. Minneapolis: Bethany House, 1990.

Associational Evangelism Council. Atlanta: Home Mission Board, 1991.

Barna, George. *User Friendly Churches*. Ventura, Calif.: Regal Books, 1991.

Beliefs of Other Kinds: A Guide to Interfaith Witness in the United States. Atlanta: Home Mission Board, 1984.

Bivocational Pastors Are Important. Atlanta: Home Mission Board, 1991.

Blanchard, Kenneth, and Spencer Johnson. *The One Minute Manager*. New York: Berkley Books, 1981.

Building Witnessing Relationships. Atlanta: Home Mission Board, 1990.

Continuing Witness Training. Atlanta: Home Mission Board, 1982.

Counselor Packet. Atlanta: Home Mission Board, 1990.

Crawford, Dan R. *Church Growth Words from the Risen Lord*. Nashville: Broadman Press, 1990.

——————————. *Families Reaching Families*. Nashville: Convention Press, 1990.

Crawford, Dan R. and C. Thomas Wright. *Total Church Life Resource Kit*. Atlanta: Home Mission Board, 1992.

Dale, Robert D. and Delos Miles. *Evangelizing the Hard-to-Reach*. Nashville: Broadman Press, 1986.

Edge, Findley B. *The Greening of the Church.* Waco, Tex.: Word Books, 1971.

Eternal Life (booklet). Atlanta: Home Mission Board, n.d.

Finley, Dean, comp. *Handbook for Youth Evangelism.* Nashville: Broadman Press, 1988.

First Steps for New Christians. Atlanta: Home Mission Board, 1990.

Good News for Everyone (booklet). Atlanta: Home Mission Board, 1991.

Good News for the Deaf (booklet). Atlanta: Home Mission Board, 1992.

Griswold, Ronald E. *The Winning Church.* Wheaton: Vic tor Books, 1986.

Hamilton, Thad. *Special Evangelistic Events Resource Kit.* Atlanta: Home Mission Board, 1991.

Harris, Richard H. *The Offer Still Stands.* Atlanta: Home Mission Board, 1991.

Hemphill, Kenneth S. *The Bonsai Theory of Church Growth.* Nashville, Broadman Press, 1991.

_____. *Spiritual Gifts: Empowering the New Testament Church.* Nashville: Broadman Press, 1988.

_____. *Mirror, Mirror on the Wall: Discovering Your True Self Through Spiritual Gifts.* Nashville: Broadman Press, 1992.

Hinson, William H. *A Place to Dig In: Doing Evangelism in the Local Church.* Nashville: Abingdon Press, 1987.

Huston, Sterling W. *Crusade Evangelism and the Local Church.* Minneapolis: World Wide Publications, 1984.

Jacks, Bob and Betty Jacks. *Your Home a Lighthouse: Hosting Evangelistic Bible Studies.* Colorado Springs: Nav Press, 1986.

Jackson, Neil L. *100 Great Growth Ideas.* Nashville: Broadman Press, 1990.

Kendall, R. T. *Stand Up and Be Counted.* Grand Rapids, Mich.: Zondervan, 1984

Leazer, Gary, and Tal Davis. *Jehovah's Witnesses: Inter*

faith Witness Associate Manual. Atlanta: Home Mission Board, 1991.

——————————. *Light on the Latter-Day Saints: Interfaith Witness Associate Manual.* Atlanta: Home Mission Board, 1991.

Lewis, Larry L. *Organize to Evangelize.* Nashville: Broadman Press, 1988.

The Marketplace Evangelism Awareness Kit. Atlanta: Home Mission Board, 1990.

The Marketplace Evangelism Church Launch Guide. Atlanta: Home Mission Board, 1990.

"Mentors in the Marketplace" (videotape). Atlanta: Home Mission Board, n.d.

One Day Soul-Winning Workshop Packet. Atlanta: Home Mission Board, 1989.

Peace, Richard. *Small Group Evangelism.* Downers Grove: InterVarsity Press, 1985.

Priority One: A Guide for Metropolitan Evangelism Strategy. Atlanta: Home Mission Board, 1985.

Revival Training Seminar Teacher's Manual. Atlanta: Home Mission Board, 1989.

Sanderson, Leonard and Ron Johnson. *Evangelism for All God's People.* Nashville: Broadman Press, 1990.

Schaller, Lyle E. *44 Ways to Increase Church Attendance.* Nashville: Abingdon Press, 1988.

Smith, Ken. *It Ought to Be Joy.* Atlanta: Home Mission Board, 1986.

Sullivan, Bill. *Ten Steps to Breaking the 200 Barrier.* Kansas City: Beacon Hill Press, 1988.

Total Church Life Video Seminar. Atlanta: Home Mission Board, 1992.

Vines, Jerry. *Wanted: Church Growers.* Nashville: Broadman Press, 1990.

Wagner, C. Peter. *Strategies for Church Growth.* Ventura, Calif.: Regal Books, 1987.

West, Sheila M. *God's People, Marketplace Style*. Monroe, Mich.: Aims Concepts, 1991.

Yousself, Michael. *Leadership Style of Jesus*. Wheaton: Victor Books, 1979.

WIN School: A Lay Evangelism Strategy. Atlanta: Home Mission Board, 1992.